FOR THE PURPOSE OF PURPOSE OF EDIFICATION

By

Rayola Kelley

Hidden **M**anna **P**ublications

For the Purpose of Edification

Copyright © 2006 and 2025 by Rayola Kelley

ISBN: 979-8-9994555-0-5

Printed in USA

Hidden Manna Publications
P.O. Box 3572
Oldtown, ID. 83822
www.gentleshepherd.com

Facebook:
https://www.facebook.com/HiddenMannaPublications/

Acknowledgment:

Many people have helped make
this book possible. I especially want to
thank Sarah Rick for her editing
and Jeannette Haley for
her proof-reading and incredible
support in helping me bring
each book to fruition.

Contents

INTRODUCTION

My reason for writing this book is to bring a balanced presentation of the gifts of the Spirit. Such a desire was born out of the reality that the discipleship group I was overseeing did not have a proper perspective of them. This aspiration to make sure that each of these disciples properly understood the gifts was in compliance with 1 Corinthians 12:1, "Now concerning spiritual gifts, brethren, I would not have you ignorant."

During the preparation for this project, I discovered that the gifts were part of a bigger picture that is often overlooked and rarely emphasized. The result of this limited picture was that gifts have become the main focal point, while their purpose or significance in the kingdom of God was totally ignored. This has caused much speculation, debate, and abuse in this area.

I began to consider the gifts in light of their purpose. They have one main function and that is to bring the Church to maturity or perfection. I also found there were other avenues that God had designed to bring the Body to maturity. Like the gifts of the Spirit, these avenues were either shrouded in debate or ignored altogether. The final result was that balanced presentations of these subjects, along with spiritual maturity, were often missing in the Body of believers.

In fact, balance is greatly missing in much of the Church because many people fail to see the larger presentation of a matter. They focus on individual parts or pieces of the depiction rather than the picture as a whole. This focus may establish theology about these subjects, but it rarely produces proper and godly practices that end in believers or a body becoming spiritually mature. What is the purpose of gifts? They are for the purpose of edification.

My prayer for this book is that it brings some balance to the controversial subjects that surround edification. I also hope that it will give hungry and thirsty Christians a sense of how far the Church has removed itself from fundamental truths that were established to bring much needed growth to believers. If one person gains a glimpse of the glorious vision of what God had in mind when Jesus died on the cross to purchase a peculiar Bride for Himself, all the time, energy, and struggles that went into writing this book will be well worth it.

1

EDIFICATION

As I tackled this project with the goal of explaining the gifts of the Spirit to bring a balanced perspective, the concept of edification repeatedly surfaced. The main purpose for certain positions and gifts in the Body of Christ is for its edification. An honest study of these gifts in light of edification will actually change how the gifts are viewed. There is clearly a broader perspective behind their purpose.

Today, debates rage over positions and gifts, but the reason God established them and gave them to the Church is never discussed at length. Granted, these positions and gifts, outside of God's reasoning for them, not only cause abuse, but also fear, ignorance, and heated debates. God did not give positions and gifts for the fun of it so people could debate, ignore, or test their personal spirituality. He gave them for the work of edification.

What is edification? A careful study of this word reveals that it has a very clear function in the Church. According to *Strong's Concordance,* this word points to building some type of structure. One might ask what structure is being constructed. Ephesians 4 and Colossians 1 make reference to Jesus' Body or Church. Peter described this spiritual structure in this way, "Ye also, as lively stones, are built as a spiritual house, an holy priesthood, to offer up spiritual sacrifices, acceptable to God by Jesus Christ" (1 Peter 2:5). The Apostle Peter clearly pointed out that there is quite a building project taking place in the kingdom of God. This process started over two millennia ago and continues today.

The writer of Hebrews also brought out this concept of building in Hebrews 3:3-6. He pointed out that Moses was faithful in his house, that the one who builds the house has more honor than the structure, and that God builds all things. Hebrews 3:6 gave this analogy, "But Christ as a son over his own house; whose house are we, if we hold fast the confidence and the rejoicing of the hope firm unto the end."

The house that is being constructed is made up of living stones or people. The Apostle Paul clearly brought this out in Romans 12:4-5, 1 Corinthians 12:12-28, and Ephesians 4:13-16.

Many Christians believe that building Christ's kingdom means building bigger church buildings. However, Jesus said in John 18:36, "My kingdom is not of this world."

The Apostle Paul made this statement in Romans 14:17, "For the kingdom of God is not meat and drink; but righteousness, and peace, and joy in the Holy Ghost." We can see that the kingdom of God is not made evident by the things that can be seen, but by that which is unseen. It is ongoing and universal in nature, and the reality of this kingdom is distinguished by the manifestation of Jesus' life in His followers.

Every structure has a design, a foundation, and a builder behind it. This spiritual building is no exception. The Father lovingly designed this spiritual structure, the Son supplied the payment for it on the cross, and the Holy Spirit is the builder.

Scripture also shows us that Jesus is the foundation and the cornerstone of this building, while Christians are the stones. The Holy Spirit is the One who properly places each stone upon the foundation, in compliance with the Cornerstone and according to the Father's eternal design.[1]

---

[1] 1 Corinthians 3:11; 1 Peter 1:19-20; 2:5-8

Each stone (Christian) has its place in this building, no matter how great or small the stone is. There is no bias or prejudice towards the significance that is placed upon each person in Jesus' Church. In fact, lively stones that are considered least by others are exalted by God to show the importance of every stone in this incredible building.[2]

As Peter stated, this is a spiritual house. This stipulates that it is not of an earthly nature, but has an eternal and heavenly function in this world. The function of this spiritual house is two-fold. First, it is to serve as a holy priesthood. Priests are meant to minister to both God and man. We see that they are to offer up spiritual sacrifices acceptable to God through Jesus Christ.

Hebrews 13:15-16 gave us insight into these sacrifices, "By him, therefore, let us offer the sacrifice of praise to God continually, that is, the fruit of our lips giving thanks to his name. But to do good and to communicate forget not, for with such sacrifices God is well pleased." These Scriptures tell us that we minister to God with praise and to others by doing good.

Sacrifices also had to have an altar. In the Old Testament tabernacle and temple, the main altar was the Altar of Burnt Offering. This was located in the outer court of the holy structure. God established this tabernacle in order to abide in the midst of Israel. Today Christians serve as the tabernacle or temple of God, and the cross of Christ serves as the altar where the sacrifice of His life was offered for all. Like the tabernacle of old, God desires to abide in the midst of the temple or, in this case, the Christian.[3]

The greater the abiding presence of God, the more distinct and holy His people will become in the midst of the world. This is the second purpose for this spiritual house—to serve as a distinct priesthood, holy nation, and peculiar people in the midst of a dark, lost world. Such a distinction will show forth the praises of Him

---

[2] 1 Corinthians 12:22-26
[3] Exodus 25:8; 1 Corinthians 3:16; Hebrews 13:10-12

who has called us out of darkness into His marvelous light to be His followers.[4]

God's main desire is to establish a spiritual house that will bring Him glory, but this house must be constructed. Christians are to serve as the stones, not the builders. In other words, Christians do not determine where they will fit in this building, nor will they place other stones into this structure. It is solely the Holy Spirit's responsibility to construct this house.

This is why Christians' perception must reach beyond doctrinal or theological views in order to embrace God's heart. His heart is simple; He wants to have a spiritual house for Himself. God's desire is often hindered because of ignorance, fear, and theological beliefs. When these culprits are on the scene, Christians cease to become the lively stones that make up this structure. At this point, Christians try to become both the designer and the builder of their spiritual lives, as well as the lives of others. This state of affairs can change the face of the Church, rendering it powerless or ineffective.

Anytime man interferes with spiritual matters, the holy becomes profane, and the vision ceases to be heavenly and becomes earthly. In the case of edification, we see where man determines spiritual practices according to theological comfort zones and emphasis, rather than the design of God. Therefore, the means of edification have become a great debate, rather than godly practices that build up the Church.

The final product is that Christians are failing to serve as stones that complement the rest of the structure. It is not unusual to see some Christians taking on the role of the Holy Spirit to determine the direction of the Church. Christians, who are trying to be the Holy Ghost, reveal that they have lost sight of the fact

---

[4] 1 Peter 2:9

that edification is not about personal beliefs, but it is the means God uses to bring believers to maturity.

The real work of edification is always about the other person being nurtured in a spiritual way and serves as a mandate to all believers. According to the Apostle Paul, all things must be done for edification; therefore, believers must avoid being caught up with things that do not edify.[5]

This proves that edification is not a matter of personal preference, but a sober responsibility of each Christian. Christians must be part of the building, rightly placed, and used by the Holy Spirit to edify others. However, to be personally part of the building, there must be self-denial and application of the cross.

The one identification mark of the Church is Jesus Christ. It must reflect His life, power, and authority. To accomplish this, Christians must become Christ-centered by coming into submission to the Holy Spirit and not self-centered nor man-centered.

The Holy Spirit does the work of edification through three avenues—positions, grace, and gifts. The Apostle Paul also talked about believers having the necessary authority and power to do the work of edification in the Body.[6] Both authority and power in this text point to positions. There have been five positions established to do the work of edification within the Church.

The number five points to grace. All work done by God within people's lives and the Church is an act of grace. Grace points not only to undeserved gifts of God, but also to an inward establishment of godliness within believers that reaches outward to others. The grace of God is meant to produce a humble attitude that results in discipline and sacrificial actions that will impact and benefit others.

---

[5] John 15:8-14; Romans 14:19; 1 Corinthians 8:1; 14:26
[6] 2 Corinthians 10:8; 13:10

The Word of God also points out that the Holy Spirit gives the necessary gifts to build the Church. The controversy surrounding gifts has practically nullified the work of edification altogether in the Church. As a result, the Body is not being built up by the power of the Spirit, but torn down by man's religious arrogance and fear.

The Apostle Paul explained the purpose of edification in Ephesians 4:13-16 as well as gave us a clear picture of how it works. Edification is to bring unity to the body. Unity of this nature comes through the knowledge and revelation of the Son of God through the Holy Ghost. This shows us that proper edification is built upon the knowledge of Jesus Christ that will produce unity in the Body.

Today there are many different Christ's being presented, and, as a result, there is no common ground or foundation. Instead of the visible Church being founded on the truth of Jesus and growing up into Him in all things, it is advocating unity at the cost of truth. This not only redefines Jesus, but also eliminates the means by which to test spiritual matters, since the real foundation will be blatantly missing.

These different "Christs" are causing many to be tossed to and fro and carried about with every wind of doctrine. This is one reason why the Church appears fragmented and vulnerable to spiritual defeat.[7] The Son of God must be perfected in a Christian before they can experience Jesus' fullness in their life. This means that certain aspects of Jesus' character or life has become a reality to and in the believer. The reality of Jesus is what constitutes real edification and unity in the Body of Christ. Such perfecting cannot be done without the love of God. Everything must be motivated and done with His love or it will fall short of edifying a person.

---

[7] Ephesians 4:14

14

This brings us to another aspect of edification; it is not always pleasant. The love of God is the motivation behind true ministers of the Gospel. This commitment has one goal and that is to see a person become mature in their life in God. This commitment may take on various forms. For example, it may show compassion to the hurting, while aggressively contending for the faith. This may mean confronting and dealing with rebellion and iniquity which rarely makes a person feel good about self or life in general. However, spiritual maturity rarely takes place without challenges, failures, and purification brought on by the various challenges of life itself along with consequences and truth.

Truth can serve as a harsh reality check to those who are hiding or justifying sin. It is meant to instruct, reprove, and correct in righteousness. When we study some of the gifts, you will begin to see that edification has a sharp edge that exposes and confronts spiritual deviation.

Another aspect of edification is that it is an ongoing work until the last lively stone is put into place. Until then, the Church is being brought to perfection or maturity. This shows us that the Church will never be completed until the Holy Spirit finishes the work, and Jesus comes for His bride.

In understanding that edification will continue until completion of the structure, one will have to conclude that the different avenues that have been established for this work will continue as well. This means that the avenues of positions and gifts will not cease until the spiritual building is finished.

Have you allowed yourself to be placed in the Body of Christ by the Holy Spirit? Are you following after that which edifies, or are you advocating that which quenches the work of the Holy Spirit?[8] Make sure you understand edification before you continue reading in order to keep this information in the proper perspective.

---

[8] Romans 14:19; 1 Thessalonians 5:19

2

THE GIVER

Once believers are exposed to the gifts, they have a tendency to pursue the gifts rather than the Giver of those gifts. Gifts do not set a person apart as a means to verify their importance in the kingdom of God, but are a medium by which God has chosen to build up the whole Body. To improperly use or over-emphasize gifts not only encourages a lopsided presentation of them, but it can cause misinformed, zealous believers to open themselves up to another spirit.

The lopsided presentation or emphasis on gifts is a product of immaturity and a misguided understanding of the Holy Spirit. This immaturity has caused many abuses of the gifts and has conditioned people to embrace that which proves contrary to the Spirit of God.

The Holy Ghost is the third person of the Godhead. He is God by nature and represents the presence and sanctifying work of God among believers of Jesus Christ. He leads to all truth about the Lord, and must be allowed to guide and lead each individual in order to accomplish the work of holiness or separation unto God.[1]

The Apostle Paul confirmed that the work of the Holy Spirit is spiritual; therefore, the natural man cannot understand, receive, or know His work because it must be spiritually discerned. Since the work of the Holy Spirit is supernatural, many become receptive

---

[1] Acts 5:3-4; Romans 15:16; John 16:13

to anything that is supernatural. This is dangerous because Satan's works are also supernatural and serve as counterfeits to the Holy Ghost and His work. Therefore, it is important to test the spirit behind any supernatural move or act to ensure that the Holy Spirit is behind it.[2]

Sadly, few know how to test the spirit. Subsequently, leaders and Christians either reject the Spirit's work or accept the wrong spirit because they are afraid to quench any type of supernatural workings, fearing that they would be quenching the Holy Spirit. These extremes have caused much confusion and debate over the Holy Spirit and His work.

E. Stanley Jones, in his devotion *The Way,* made this comment about the first group, "The almost entire absence of emphasis on the Spirit has impoverished the main stream of Christianity. It often degenerates into a humanistic striving to be good."

The other group abuses the Holy Spirit, along with His gifts, because they do not know His character. They live in fear that they are quenching His work. This ignorance has allowed Satan to effectively counterfeit the Holy Spirit and His works in the midst of many Christians and congregations. This has caused destructive spiritual mixtures that profane the holy. Therefore, it is vital that people who desire to experience the Holy Spirit in a greater measure understand His character.

The character of the Holy Spirit can be realized in His work and the many symbols that point to Him. In Genesis 1:2, He moved upon the face of the earth to bring order through recreation. In all of His workings, there will be order and not chaos. In many of these meetings where the supernatural is working, order is missing, and it seems like there are no boundaries to the different manifestations. Therefore, much is being embraced as originating from the Spirit of God, when it is nothing but a counterfeit. The

---

[2] 1 Corinthians 2:14; 1 John 4:1

truth is that legitimate moves of God will not operate outside of the character of the Holy Ghost. His very character demands a clear order and reverent conduct and an attitude of worship.

In Genesis 2:6, the Holy Spirit was symbolized by the mist that went up from the earth that revived that which was unproductive. We see this similar example of His work in the spiritual birth. He is the breath of God that brings life to a lifeless soul, as well as the Living Water that cleanses and brings restoration to the parched soul.[3]

In Genesis 8:8, He was the dove sent forth by Noah (a type of Father God) from the ark (a type of Jesus) to explore the condition of the terrain (a type of man's heart).[4] In the case of the Church, the Holy Spirit can only move and land upon that which is prepared and holy.

He is gentle and can easily be quenched, causing Him to quickly withdraw.[5] He tests the spiritual temperature of God's Church and determines if the Church is prepared for His move and work. If He encounters sin, that which is fleshly, or the wrong spirit, He will lift and return to the Father until He is sent again to test the terrain. After all, it is God's heart to move upon His people in a powerful way. It is during such a move that He will sovereignly meet people in their spiritual plights as He distributes gifts, comforts, and reveals the heart of God to the searching, humble heart.

We see the third person of the Godhead descending like a dove after the baptism of Jesus Christ at the River Jordan. The Holy Ghost always illuminates the reality of Jesus in the midst of His Body, the Church. In fact, His main responsibility is to lead a

---

[3] John 3:3-6; 7:37-39

[4] There are many types in the Old Testament. These types serve as an example or representation of someone or something. The greatest type is the tabernacle, which serves as one of the greatest revelations of Jesus Christ—His nature, purpose, and ministry.

[5] 1 Thessalonians 5:19

person into the truth about the Son of God.[6] If Jesus is not being lifted up in a meeting or movement, the Holy Spirit will be absent as well.

In Genesis 8:1, the Holy Spirit was represented by the powerful wind that passed over the earth to push back judgment in order to bring forth the promises of God and a new beginning for man. All men stand condemned because of sin, but if any man gives way to the reality of Christ, the Holy Spirit comes in to push back judgment and bring forth new life. He then serves as the seal in the lives of believers, making them heirs to an eternal inheritance.[7]

Jesus also referred to the Holy Spirit as the wind that man couldn't explain or control in John 3:7-8. As already mentioned, He is the very breath of God in a new creation's life. But He is also ascribed as being the wind. He came as a rushing wind on the day of Pentecost that not only stirred up the fire that had been slowly burning in the hearts of Jesus' followers, but He also caused it to spread as they became powerful witnesses of the Gospel.[8]

Genesis 24 presents the trustworthy servant (a type of the Holy Ghost) sent out by Abraham (a type of Father God) to find a bride (a type of Church) for his son, Isaac (a type of Jesus, the Son of Man). In this powerful story, we can learn that the Holy Spirit does not represent or promote Himself. He acts in accordance with the Father, and His main goal is to find a bride, adorn her with jewels, woo her to the Son, and lead her back to dwell with her bridegroom. This picture shows that He will not act outside of God's design, and He will always glorify Jesus, not Himself. If a person rejects His overtures, the Holy Ghost will be released from all responsibilities, but He will be greatly grieved.[9]

---

[6] Matthew 3:16; John 16:13-14
[7] Ephesians 1:11-14
[8] Acts 2:2-7
[9] Ephesians 4:30

In the building of the tabernacle, we see at least three representations of the Holy Spirit. His character can be observed in Bezaleel, a man from the tribe of Judah. It was out of the tribe of Judah that Jesus would come forth, and it is because of the Holy Spirit that Jesus is made a reality to His followers.

Bezaleel is the man who was filled with the wisdom, understanding, and knowledge to build the tabernacle. The Holy Spirit is the essence of all knowledge, understanding, wisdom, and revelation among Jesus' followers. He resides in the temple of man and, as a result, He can make the Church a living, active reality that is able to express the very image of Christ to the world. He is the One who makes a dead soul alive unto God by regenerating the person.[10] He places each believer in the Body and makes the head, Jesus Christ, a passion that cannot be quenched, a reality that cannot be denied, and the very source of a person's heartbeat.

Bezaleel's helper, Aholiab, points to the work of the Holy Ghost among the believers, specifically the gifts of the Spirit. Aholiab was from the tribe of Dan, which means "judge." The gifts not only edify, but also serve as a type of judgment to bring separation from that which is unholy. God often uses the gifts as a means to instruct, exhort, and warn in order to bring such separation.[11]

Author and teacher, Ruth Specter Lascelle, pointed out certain aspects about Bezaleel and Aholiab. Bezaleel was from Judah. Judah was the leading camp when Israel was traveling through the wilderness, while Dan, Aholiab's tribe, was the last camp of Israel. We are to follow after the Spirit, be led by the Spirit, and walk in the Spirit. Clearly, as believers, He is to be in front of us, in our midst, and surrounding us. As part of the first and last, these two men stand as representatives of the complete camp. Lascelle pointed out that the gifts of the Holy Spirit (followed after Jesus'

---

[10] Exodus 35:30-31; Ephesians 1:17; 1 Corinthians 3:16; Titus 3:5
[11] Exodus 35:34-35

ascension) and the "ministry" gifts go together with Jesus (the head).[12] The completion of this combination of these works and gifts points to the edification and perfecting of the whole Body.

The next representatives of the Holy Spirit in the work of the tabernacle are the anointing oil and spices.[13] Oil represents the anointing of the Holy Spirit, while the spices symbolize His work through Christ and the believer.[14] There are five ingredients in this anointing oil, which point to the work of grace. Bezaleel originally prepared this oil, showing that only the Holy Spirit can combine the right ingredients in man's life and in the Church to make both holy and acceptable to God.[15] This oil was used to set people, objects, sacrifices, and places apart for God's use and glory.

How well do you know the character of the Holy Spirit? Is He simply a doctrine that you control or a comfortable concept that never challenges your ignorance about Him and His work? It is vital that you allow the Spirit to shake you as He did those in the upper room, so you can personally experience the third person of the Godhead in an intimate, powerful way.

Receiving the Promise

There are many misconceptions about how a person receives the Holy Spirit. Many believe if they want more of the Holy Spirit, they must personally seek Him out. There is no Scripture to back up this concept.

The Word clearly states that the Holy Spirit is a gift that cannot be earned and a promise that must be given.[16] Jesus Christ is the one who gives the Holy Spirit to the believer as a gift, while the

---

[12] A Dwelling Place for God by Ruth Specter Lascelle; © 1990 by Hyman Israel Specter, Van Nuys CA.
[13] Exodus 30:23-25; Luke 4:18-19
[14] A Dwelling Place for God; pages 343-345
[15] Exodus 31:11; 37:29
[16] Luke 24:49; Acts 1:4; 8:17-20

Father provides the promise by sending Him forth to do a work among believers.

There are two distinct ways by which Jesus gives the Holy Spirit. The first act occurs when a believer is born again. We see Jesus giving His disciples the Holy Spirit before He ascended to heaven.[17] This was the example of the born-again experience, but this only occurred after Gethsemane and Calvary. In other words, spiritual birth is marked by self-denial and death (the cross of Christ) to ensure life. This birth implies that the presence of God is within the spirit of man.

The next distinct act happened at Pentecost. The disciples had the Spirit, but they were told to wait until they were endued with power from on high.[18] They waited for seven days for the Father's promise of the Spirit. On the seventh day, Jesus took the promise and made Him the gift with which He baptized the believers with Living Water from above. This Water would subdue all residues of self and empower His followers to live righteous lives, as well as serve as bold witnesses for His kingdom.

E. Stanley Jones explained the difference between the new birth and the fullness of the Holy Spirit, "Before Pentecost the disciples had the Holy Spirit, but after Pentecost the Holy Spirit had them."[19]

It was at Pentecost that the Presence of God from within connected with the power from on high to raise each believer up to testify of the new life from within with power and authority. These people became living epistles of God's love that was displayed on the cross. They spoke with authority because they carried with them the mark of death, and displayed power because of the resurrected life that pulsated through their very being.

---

[17] John 20:22:23
[18] Luke 24:48-49; Acts 1:4-8
[19] The Way, E. Stanley Jones, devotional, pg. 274

This brings us back to the subject of how we can receive this power. Do we seek the Holy Spirit to receive a greater measure of Him? Scripture is very clear that we are not to seek out the Holy Spirit because He is not here to give Himself to us. He is a promise from the Father; therefore, we must ask the Father for more of the Spirit of the Living God. Luke 11:13 confirmed this, "If ye then, being evil, know how to give good gifts unto your children: how much more shall your heavenly Father give the Holy Spirit to them that ask him?"

The Father desires us to ask Him for His Holy Spirit, but our motives must be right. We must not ask the Father for the Holy Ghost so that we can have gifts that will bring us recognition, but so that we can have the power to bring Him glory. After all, the Holy Spirit's main motive is to shed love abroad in the believer's heart towards God and others. His intent is to bring glory to God, and His goal is to lift Jesus above the world, fleshly desires, and Satan's designs to serve as an invitation to the seeking, despairing heart.

The Father waits for us to ask Him for the Holy Spirit, while Jesus waits for us to come to Him, so that He can give us more of the Spirit to fulfill His many promises to His Bride. The ring in the parable of the Prodigal Son represents the Holy Spirit. This ring is a seal that shows that one belongs to a particular household. For the Christian, they belong to the kingdom of God, and the seal of the Holy Spirit guarantees each one an eternal inheritance.[20]

Interestingly, the early Christian writers referred to the filling of the Holy Spirit as the Lord's seal. They believed that the born-again experience was where the new Christian became the possession of the Lord. But, the sealing of Christians was like

---

[20] Luke 15:22; Ephesians 1:11-14

23

putting a brand on them just as a man might brand the sheep that were already His.[21]

This reminds us that the whole goal of the Holy Ghost is to exalt Jesus in everything. When a believer comes to Jesus, seeking to possess Him in a greater reality, they receive a greater measure of the Holy Ghost. Jesus confirmed this in John 7:37-39,

> Jesus stood and cried, saying, If any man thirst, let him come unto me, and drink. He that believeth on me as the scripture hath said, out of his belly shall flow rivers of living water. (But this spake he of the Spirit, which they that believe on him should receive: for the Holy Ghost was not yet given; because that Jesus was not yet glorified.) (Emphasis added.)

It is important to understand the character and work of the Spirit as the third Person of the Godhead. The following tables reveals the work of each person in relationship to each other:

Person	Point of Identification (2 Cor. 13:14)	Creation	Expression	Means of Salvation
The Father	*Love* (1 Jn. 3:1)	*Designer* (1 Cor 8:6)	*Prophets/Son* (He. 1:1-2)	*Draws* Jn. 6:44
The Son	*Grace* (Jn. 1:16)	*Builder/Creator* (Col. 1:15-18; Heb. 11:3)	*The Word* (Jn. 1:1; He. 11:3; Ps. 148:5)	*Invites* (Jn. 7:37-39)
Holy Spirit	*Communion* (Jn. 4:23-24)	*Finish/Recreates* (Ge. 1:2; Jb. 26:13)	*The Ink* (2 Co. 3:3)	*Convicts* (Jn. 16:7-11)
Believer	*New Life* (Ga. 2:20)	*New Creation* (2 Co. 5:17)	*The Letter* (2 Co. 3:2)	*Believes* (Ro. 10:9-10)

---

[21] Deeper Experiences of Famous Christians, James Gilchrist Lawson, © 2000 by Barbour Publishing, Inc.

The Father is the One who designs, ordains, and establishes the way a matter must be. He sets forth the plan and pre-ordains how it will be brought forth for His glory. Everything the Son and the Holy Spirit do is in line with the Father's design, plan, and purpose.

Person	Goal of Salvation	Plan	Manifestation	Purpose
The Father	Reconciliation (Eph. 1:10; 2:16)	Do His Will (Mt. 12:46-50)	Relationship (Jn. 1:12)	Fellowship (1 Jn 1:3)
The Son	Redemption (Eph. 1:7)	Have His Mind (Phil. 2:5)	The Place (1 Co. 1:30)	Citizenship (Ep. 2:19)
The Holy Spirit	Born Again (Jn. 3:3, 5)	Empower (Acts 1:7-8)	Sanctification (1 Pe. 1:2)	Inheritance (Ep. 1:13-14)
Believer	Adoption (Ep. 1:5)	Method (Mt. 28:18-20)	Consecration (Ro. 12:1)	Identification (Ro. 6:4-5)

God's plan has always been about restoring the relationship that was lost in the Garden of Eden. To restore what was lost, there would have to be a point of reconciliation. The place of reconciliation can only occur upon redemption. It is for this reason the Father exalts the Son, the Son was lifted up, and the Holy Spirit leads people to Jesus because He is the only one who can bring forth reconciliation. We can get caught up with many great truths, but the red thread that runs through Scripture from the old to the new is redemption.[22]

[22] 2 Corinthians 5:18-21; Philippians 2:9-11; John 12:32; 16:13

Person	Communica-tion	Prayer	Desire	Church
The Father	*Worship* (Jo. 4:23)	*As Father* (Mt. 6:9)	*Communion* (Ex. 25:22)	*Administrator* (1 Co. 12:6)
The Son	*Shepherd* (Jn. 10:14)	*Covenant* (Jn. 14:6, 13)	*Friendship* Jn. 15:14-15	*All in All* Col. 3:11
The Holy Spirit	*Revelation* (Ep. 3:3)	*Inspiration* (Ep. 6:18)	*Unity* (Ep. 4:3)	*Edifier* (Ep. 4:12)
Believer	*Disciple* (Mt. 16:24)	*Instrument* (Ro. 6:13)	*Know Him* (Phil. 3:10)	*Lively Stones* (1 Pe. 2:5)

As you can see, these tables are just touching the surface. You can take any subject and do a study and find out how all three persons of the Godhead were or are involved. We know all three persons of the Godhead were involved with the resurrection of Christ. Take the subject of gifts. *James 1:17* tells us every perfect gift comes from the Father and *Ephesians 1:7* tells us Jesus is that gift while we are told in *1 Corinthians 12:7-11* that the Holy Spirit is the one who gives the gifts for edification of the Body to whom He will. The Apostle Paul speaks of great gratitude and awe towards the gift he has been given by referring to it as the unspeakable gift.[23]

As we can see, without the Holy Spirit there is no life, worship, or true service when it comes to the Kingdom of God. We need to be filled with the Spirit daily to ensure His sanctifying of our service, transforming of the mind, and renewing of the spirit.

When was the last time you asked the Father for more of the Spirit, so that you can live a life pleasing to Him? When did you last come to Jesus, seeking more of Him, only to be given more of the Holy Ghost? Do not seek the Spirit for more of His abiding presence and power. Rather, believe what the Word says and respond in simple child-life faith, knowing God wants you to have more of the presence of His Spirit in your life.

---

[23] John 2:19-21; Romans 8:11; 2 Corinthians 9:15; Galatians 1:1

3

THE DESIGN

The Body of Christ is meant to function as a fine-tuned organism, void of division. To ensure unity in this Body, there is only one body, one Spirit, one calling, one Lord, one faith, one baptism, and one God. This Body has one head, is established on one immovable foundation, and is lined up to one cornerstone, Jesus Christ.[1]

Five positions were instituted to line the Church up to the leadership of Jesus and establish it on the right foundation— apostles, prophets, evangelists, pastors, and teachers. The Apostle Paul made reference to all of these positions in Ephesians 4:11 and to some of them in 1 Corinthians 12:28.

It is important to put these positions in the right perspective because there has been much erroneous teaching and abuse about this subject, especially in the areas of apostles and prophets. Much of this violation has to do with Ephesians 2:20, "And are built upon the foundation of the apostles and prophets, Jesus Christ himself being the chief corner stone."

This Scripture shows that the apostles and prophets initially established the foundation of the Church, but it was always in line with the Person of Jesus Christ. Everything these individuals established as foundational truths and everything they instructed and maintained in written epistles was in line with the spirit,

---

[1] Matthew 21:42-44; Ephesians 4:3-6; 1 Corinthians 3:11; Colossians 1:15-18

character, example, and teachings of Jesus Christ. Not only were these teachings to serve as immovable truths, but they also contained within them great treasures that could be discovered by those who were sincere and child-like in heart.[2]

Once these treasures were uncovered, they would reveal a greater revelation of Jesus Christ. It is important to point out that the apostles and prophets who initially laid the foundation were not establishing new revelations. Rather, they were embellishing on a revelation that had been hidden until unveiled in Jesus Christ. This is why Jesus Christ is the only spiritual foundation and cornerstone.[3] Every teaching must be founded in Him and be in line with His character and example.

In his book *Will the Real Heretics Please Stand Up*, David W. Bercot explained how the early Church maintained pure doctrine. The new Church had to contend with many counterfeit epistles or letters. Apparently, it was the early Christians who depended on the guidance of the Holy Spirit to determine which letters were genuine. Once the New Testament was in place, the attitude of the believers from that point on was that there would be no special doctrinal revelations beyond the foundation that was established by the prophecies of the Old Testament prophets and the teachings of the first apostles and prophets.

For the first three centuries, Christians maintained this strong stand in regards to any other presentations of doctrine. This strong stand protected the purity of truth and doctrines as well as maintained the intent of the Word. Since the channel had been preserved in relationship to purity of God's Word, people could be led to a greater revelation of Jesus Christ.

The doctrinal wall of protection began to especially erode away in the fourth century when the pursuit for purity of doctrine and separation from the world changed to unifying the different

---

[2] Colossians 2:2-3
[3] 1 Corinthians 3:11; Ephesians 1:17; 2:20

religious beliefs under one "Christian" auspice. This concept sounded wonderful to the Christians who had suffered various types of persecution for over two centuries, but, in the end, it robbed the Church of its authority and power.

I have no doubt that, in the fourth century, this new zeal over having a "Christian" world, blinded well-meaning Christians to the harsh reality that Christians were not meant to come into unity with the world, but to attract lost souls out of it to Jesus Christ. As one of the illustrations found in *Encyclopedia of Sermon Illustrations* pointed out: "If the church joins the world, there is no need for the world to join the church." Today, we see this same trend to bring the world under a "Christian" umbrella even though history proves it to be disastrous.

We see where Christians today are more politically minded than spiritually inclined in their pursuits for personal holiness. As a result, there is no distinction between the world and the Church. Christians are busy trying to change governments, laws, and policies rather than contending for souls in order to see changed hearts and lives. In fact, they are in the business of conforming people to a moral standard, instead of upholding that which transforms the carnal mind in its enmity against God.[4]

The early Christians failed to realize the danger of unity with this unholy combination. It meant compromising truth and implementing a leadership that would establish perverted doctrines. Initially, these leaders were not given the titles of apostles and prophets in the first couple of centuries, but they were placed into the same type of positions in order to redefine the foundation laid by the first apostles.

As the walls of protection crumbled, the Church became open to the creeds of men to redefine foundational truths and doctrines, often exceeding the norm or negating the authority of the written Word. As men's traditions and superstitions invaded the Church,

---

[4] Romans 8:7-8; 12:1-2

issues such as holiness, repentance, faith, and grace were redefined, causing many to become blind to the spirit or complete counsel of Scripture. As they became blind to foundational truths, they lost sight of the real Jesus.

This breakdown caused men to become reliant on man to interpret the Word rather than on the Holy Spirit. Such alliance put basic truths and doctrinal issues into the arena of intellectual pursuits, endless debates, and higher criticism. Men began to debate the legitimacy of some of the New Testament books, while embracing certain gospels or epistles that corresponded to their beliefs. What started out as an attempt to bring unity ended in division, denominations, and disillusioned people. Instead of people becoming followers of Jesus, they became followers of a person and preferred beliefs, making them promoters of men's traditions rather than fulfilling their commission to preach the Gospel of Jesus Christ.

Through the years, these traditions and so-called "revelations" have been added to the religious state of the Church. Different denominations and cults have mushroomed, drowning out the simplicity of Christ and watering down the Gospel. These beliefs have become the final authority to what many believe.

In this last century, the Church has seen the rise of countless self-proclaimed apostles and prophets. These positions have been exalted as ranks, making the people who hold such titles the final authority. These people are claiming to have new revelations that cleverly undermine the foundational truths and doctrines of Christianity. They have subtly changed the face of Christianity by presenting another Jesus, promoting another gospel, and operating under another spirit. They have accomplished this by exalting a few "elite" men as the "anointed ones" or "messiahs."[5]

---

[5] 2 Corinthians 11:1-11

These self-proclaimed leaders advocate faith in man and encourage blind allegiance to their leadership, as these imposters are often exalted as God in the eyes of their followers. They are arrogant, demanding, and some have become rich at the expense of their blind subjects.

The victims of this movement are the local bodies of believers. Many unsuspecting Christians have lost their heavenly vision as they became lost in a maze of expensive mega-churches. This has caused many to accept counterfeits as they became caught up with the fleshly hypes and different religious movements that are ecumenical in nature.

This ecumenism is a means of trying to unify the true, universal Church under the auspices of the new breed of apostles and prophets. Sadly, this unity is moving the Church into the heretical, dangerous one-world religion that has been prophesied in the Word of God.

It is important to point out that the New Testament apostles and prophets were placed in a position and not in leadership roles. Positions determine responsibility and imply an official capacity. For example, the official capacity of apostles and prophets was to establish the Church on the right foundation and ensure all growth was in line with Jesus Christ. Their activities were not to exceed the norm of their official capacity, such as taking over the leadership of the local bodies. Keep in mind, many apostles traveled from place to place to establish or edify the different local bodies. Once the local churches were in place, these apostles continued to instruct through epistles, while working among other bodies of believers. We see this in the lives of Paul and Peter.

Leadership of local bodies was given to individuals who worked within the local church and were recognized by their godliness and spiritual wisdom. These believers had to fit strict criteria. They were individuals who were often financially poor, but were rich in faith and the knowledge of Jesus Christ. They were meek and lowly in spirit and knew how to count the cost. The reason for this is because these pillars were the first to be targeted when persecution raised its fist against local churches. They were believers who had to be dead to the world and alive unto God. They cared only for the reality of Jesus and being faithful to the sheep that were entrusted to them. These saints were referred to as elders (bishops) and deacons, not apostles and prophets.[6]

These leaders of the New Testament Church ensured accountability on a local level, but those of the local body also held them accountable. We clearly see this in the instruction the Apostle Paul gave Timothy in 1 Timothy 5:19-20. Sadly, today these leadership positions are either being compromised, abused for personal gain and exaltation, or whittled down to a title with no real meaning or responsibility in the Church.

This undermining of leadership has caused the Church to become vulnerable to wolves in sheep's clothing. I have no doubt many of these wolves are masquerading as ministers (apostles and prophets) of righteousness to steal sheep away from the local bodies.[7]

The main goal of these wolves is financial gain. They are making merchandise of people's souls with vain words and promises.[8] Their foolish covetousness will bring greater damnation on them. In the meantime, the sheep are being isolated, wounded, and, in some cases, destroyed by these wolves. As unsuspecting people support these wolves, the real work of God is overlooked and greatly hindered. In short, these wolves are robbing from the real servants of God.

The positions and gifts were given for the edification of the Body and not for the promotion of a few self-appointed leaders. Godly leaders are humble servants who do not merchandise God

---

[6] See 1 Timothy 3:1-13; 5:17-20; Titus 1:5-9; James 2:5
[7] Matthew 7:15; Acts 29:29
[8] See John 2:16; 2 Peter 2:3

or His sheep for personal prestige and gain. They are not trying to sell any goods for personal gain; rather, their heart desire is to exemplify the Person of Jesus in attitude and actions. They are not trying to promote the Gospel with enticing words or worldly means, but "in power and with the Holy Ghost."[9]

These counterfeits require that a distinction be made by believers between false leaders and the positions that were established for the benefit and growth of the Church. As you examine this distinction, ask yourself if you have bought the lies from any of the many wolves that are parading around in the name of God.

---

[9] 1 Thessalonians 1:5

4

THE POSITIONS

Positions in the kingdom of God do not point to rank; rather, they represent an act of placing a person in a proper order to fulfill God's purpose or design. This concept is made obvious when one considers how every Christian is not only personally placed within the Body of Christ, but placed by God in Christ. We also know that the placing of individuals is not an attempt by God to exalt a few over the masses because God is no respecter of persons. In fact, His order within the Body of Christ exalts members that seem insignificant in the scheme of things to equal footing and importance in His kingdom.[1]

This equality is due to the fact that everyone is a sinner and stands equally in need of forgiveness and salvation. Such equality does away with superiority and elitism, the very attitudes that cause competition, division, and resentment among people.

This brings us back to who is the greatest in the kingdom of God? Is greatness in God's sight the same as in the world? Sadly, many Christians consider greatness in light of the world and not according to Scripture.

The world determines greatness based on titles and degrees. It matters little to most people if the person fits the title in practical skills as long as the degrees, certificates, and education confirm that the person has rights to declare such honors.

---

[1] Acts 10:34; 1 Corinthians 1:30; 12:23-24

In the kingdom of God, greatness is not determined by position, but by attitude and action. According to Jesus, the greatest in the kingdom of God is a servant of all.[2] A servant is humble in attitude, submissive in action, and obedient in practice. Such servants have given up rights and given way to a worthy authority. Servants are not here to serve their personal pursuits, but those of their master.

The disposition of servitude and a sincere and sacrificial love for the Master is what sets all great leaders apart in God's kingdom. These leaders have no personal agendas outside of Christ and Him crucified.[3] They stand for truth, contend for one true faith, and are singular in vision. They are led by the Spirit, compelled by godly love, and heaven bound. They are sojourners who are crucified to the world and possess one main goal of finishing the course to gain and possess the ultimate reward of heaven, Jesus Himself.

Today there are many claiming titles in the kingdom of heaven, but few can rightfully lay claim to them. These counterfeits lack the disposition and fruits that would confirm that they are legitimate.

This brings us to the subject of the positions that were established for the purpose of properly building the Church. Those who will ultimately possess greatness in God's kingdom will not do so on the basis of these positions, but because they have a disposition of a real servant. Individuals who declare their legitimacy based on titles alone are those who are fraudulent in their claims. Those who are frauds will lack the heart and attitude of a servant and will be void of the life of Christ.

It is the life of Christ that serves as the light within the soul of man. If this light is present, it will reveal the mind of Christ. If this

---

[2] Matthew 20:25-27
[3] 1 Corinthians 2:2

light is absent, it reveals that the person is self-serving and a servant of the kingdom of darkness.

With this in mind, let us now consider the positions that were established for the Church's benefit.

Apostles

According to *Strong's Exhaustive Concordance,* "apostle" means an official delegate, ambassador of Christ, or sent out one. As an official representative of the kingdom God, this individual is commissioned to take one consistent message to each kingdom, country, or nation that they are sent to. The message is known as the Gospel, the power of God unto salvation.[4]

As you can see, the implications of a modern-day apostle are not to redefine or establish a new foundation, but to officially represent the King of kings and the Lord of lords wherever they are to go. Usually, these people start new local churches wherever they are called. Once a work is started, these servants must ensure that Christ is the foundation and cornerstone to every soul that is being placed within the local church or body for the work and glory of God. After all, each member makes up a lively priesthood, a spiritual house.[5]

Because of the confusion and misuse of the word apostle, the Church has devised another term that would embrace the work of the apostle—missionary. A missionary is sent to other places to represent Jesus as ambassadors. These people's responsibilities may vary according to the needs of those around them, but like the first apostles, they can find themselves establishing local bodies through preaching, teaching, contending for souls and truth, and serving as a light in dark places.

---

[4] Romans 1:16
[5] 1 Peter 2:5

36

The work of the apostle or missionary may last only a season. The Holy Spirit may move these servants on to another work or change their present status by redefining their work according to the needs and the direction of the new church. These servants of God must be capable of showing love, flexibility, patience, and obedience to any change of direction in God's work. As a result, their greatest contribution to the kingdom of God often becomes their example of devotion, sacrifice, and sincerity to do God's bidding wherever they are planted.

Prophets

These people are known to operate in two areas—foretelling (warning others of future events) and forthtelling (preaching and exhortation). The apostles establish the local church, but prophets are responsible to guard the spirit of the new church and maintain it in righteousness.

The problem with this position is that many wolves have hid behind the position of prophet.[6] The reason this position is so attractive is because of the prophetic implications. Even though the position of prophet has a greater responsibility than foretelling future events, many people are drawn to the prophetic and can be easily deceived by false prophets.

Although the greatest Prophet of history, Jesus Christ, pretty much covered the last days in an extensive way, these modern-day false prophets are running around with a word for every person, city, nation, and country operating as fortunetellers, rather than foretelling according to the Spirit of God. Many of their words are generic and fleshly.

This is important to note because a genuine prophet will give prophecies that can be tested by specific details and will not have to be stretched in any fashion to make it appear genuine like the

---

[6] Matthew 7:15-16

counterfeits do. The genuine prophet will always point people to Jesus Christ and never exalt self as the only legitimate voice of God that people must trust.

On the other hand, false prophets may call people to repentance and holiness, but never to Jesus Christ. They subtly exalt themselves to the place of a religious expert and eventually take center stage as "the anointed one" or "messiah".

The false prophet ultimately fails to fulfill this position because the main concern of genuine prophets is to prepare others for the coming of Jesus. These dedicated servants are to make the path straight for the Holy Spirit to move freely to unveil Christ to seeking hearts. This is where preaching, warning, and exhortation will become the tools they use to contend for the spiritual growth and wholeness of the Church.

In order to prepare His people, God gives prophets discernment. They will discern the spirit or intent behind leaders, doctrines, and movements. They will display sensitivity to the Spirit and will only speak under His inspiration. As a result, they are able to take up the sword of the Word and impart it with power and authority. As the sword becomes powerful and living, the motives and intents of others will be exposed.

Since darkness resents light according to the religious counterfeit, godly prophets are unpopular. They will insist on purity, rather than popularity and money. They will reprove sin, stand against heresy, silence foolishness, and take an axe to all roots and practices of idolatry. They will prove to be bold for truth, as well as relentless soldiers of the cross, and will have a no-nonsense approach towards all deception. As a result, prophets are unattractive to the religious masses and travel a lonely road of separation like Jeremiah and John the Baptist.

Because of the skepticism caused by false prophets, the Church, once again, has given these people another name—watchmen. We see this term was used in the case of the prophet,

Ezekiel.[7] God also made a reference between the righteous watchmen and the false prophets in Hosea 9:8.

It is important to note that the prophet is not always obvious. They might be the unassuming person sitting next to you in the pew. Like the prophet Amos, a true prophet can only respond when God calls them, and God might only call the individual once to warn His Body of heresy, trouble, or pending judgment. The initial response by most to a true prophet of God is to ignore, discredit, or silence their voice instead of testing the warning or exhortation. If you discover a person is a false prophet, contend with the person. But, if you find the saying or warning of the prophet is true, respond in humility, submission, and obedience or judgment will follow.

Evangelist

When we think of an evangelist, we envision a person who is preaching fire and damnation behind pulpits, in tents, and on the streets. Granted, an evangelist reaches out to the unsaved, but the individual who holds this position is also responsible for the edification of the Church.

Apostles establish new churches upon the right foundation and line them up to the Cornerstone. The prophets guard the Church against heresy and call members to scriptural accountability. But the evangelists are responsible for challenging and enlarging the vision of the Church.

Christianity is a spiritual kingdom existing within worldly kingdoms and nations. As a result, Christians are called to be separate from the world. Believers who live separate from the world ensure a powerful testimony that enables them to carry out their commission—to preach the Gospel and make new converts followers of Christ. This commission serves as the Church's vision

---

[7] Ezekiel 3:17; 33:7

in the world. It is supernatural and heavenly, as well as laying at the heart of God and the Church's purpose for being in the world.

A church without this vision becomes like the Dead Sea, where much fresh water is taken in, but none of it is given out. This type of church will be good at taking from the resources of others, but it fails to become a conduit from which the Living Water flows to others. This condition causes stagnation, which produces spiritual dullness. Spiritual dullness translates to indifference to souls and a slumbering local church that will fail to carry out its commission.

This is where the evangelist becomes part of the edification of the body. They must stir the church out of its spiritual slumber to once again consider the purpose for being in the world—to preach the Gospel and make disciples of Jesus. This stirring means a renewing or reviving of the church. In order to accomplish this, the evangelist has to be empowered with the Holy Spirit and must shake the church out of its comfort zone with inspired preaching from the throne room of God. The main call of the evangelist will not be for Christians to fulfill their commission, but to repent for failing to do so.

The absence of the Church's heavenly vision displays disobedience and a lack of godly love. It takes the love of God to properly respond to the commission. Once the Church repents of its wicked ways of unbelief and of being lukewarm and adheres to the commission, it is being obedient to the Word of God. Therefore, the evangelist must revive not only the vision, but also a love for God. This is why these individuals must have the inspiration of the Holy Spirit. Only the Spirit of God can cause repentance that will translate into a fire of revival and fervor that will not only cause the church to rise up in boldness, but fan the fire of devotion and boldness in the hearts of others.

Sadly, evangelists are becoming a rare breed in America. In the 1800's and early 1900's, evangelists held meetings that lasted for weeks. This allowed the evangelist to tear down idolatry, root-out disobedience, and properly challenge people in order to build up the local church. It gave time for the Holy Spirit to prepare, move, break, restore, and save souls. It encouraged both the saved and the unsaved to do business with God until the person knew God's will and direction for their life.

These meetings were eventually cut down from weeks to days and, finally, to a few meetings a week. Apparently, the church became too busy to commit to weeks of intense spiritual examination. The reasons vary, but one of the biggest reasons, besides a loss of vision and the instant society mentality, is entertainment.

Evangelistic meetings used to be the main attraction in town for believers, but now believers can be exposed to all the Christian influences they need via radio and television. They can sit and partake of various religious themes and be professionally entertained at the same time. They can become emotionally hyped without getting real about what is going on in their hearts and lives. They can tack a religious cloak on and deem all is good without coming to repentance. They can walk in a religious fantasy, while ignoring their commission.

The main difference between these two avenues of evangelistic meetings and religious entertainment is the personal touch. People can be indifferent to personal spiritual problems because there is no accountability when it comes to the media. After all, the Holy Spirit wants to personally meet with the individual to expose hidden problems and sins, as well as encourage and build up. These different medias allow for the religious conscience to be soothed while hiding sins beneath a religious cloak. This atmosphere encourages a feel-good religion without any substance or power behind it.

God uses man to be an extension of His heart, voice, hands, and feet. There is something about a personal touch and encounter that encourages and allows healing and restoration to take place in a weary soul.

Another reason the evangelist is becoming a dying breed in America is because of the attitude of some church leaders towards this position. I had one pastor tell me he did not need an evangelist to come to his church because he was all his church needed. The doors of his church are now closed, silently mocking his high evaluation of himself and his blatant disregard for the Word of God. The Bible clearly states that evangelists are part of God's plan of edification for the Body, and true leaders of God will not brush such a reality to the side.

An international evangelist gave me another aspect of the challenges that buffet evangelists. He stated that most leaders of churches, especially in America, are only interested in numbers and not souls. He shared with me that, if an evangelist failed to get the numbers of people up to the altar, they were not asked back.

This has placed evangelists in a competitive role, rather than a contender for souls. Evangelists have to resort to manipulative and controlling practices to get people to the altars, whether their repentance or rededication is sincere or not.

I remember attending an evangelistic meeting where I never heard one word preached from the Word, but instead witnessed a variety of manipulative approaches by the evangelist to get people to respond to his call for them to come to the altar. I became repulsed by his methods and left the meeting early.

Much of the evangelism going on is pleasing to the ears, stirring up emotions, and entertaining, but the power of the Spirit and Gospel is missing. It stirs up the flesh, rather than the spirit. It sets "self" aflame with good feelings, rather than obtaining a heavenly vision that burns for lost souls.

The apostle, prophet, and evangelist are not permanent positions within the local church. People who hold these positions either travel or have their responsibilities redefined by the condition or needs of the local body of believers. People who hold these positions must be flexible and sojourners at heart. They are often hidden in obscurity, ready to respond to God's call to be broken vessels and poured out like wine for the benefits of others and the glory of God.

Now that we have considered the versatile positions of the Church, let us examine the two permanent positions found in the local bodies.

5

A SERVANT OF ALL

While the positions of apostles, prophets, and evangelists can be temporary, changing, or even obscure to the rest of the body, the last two positions in Ephesians 4:11 remain constant within the Body of Christ. This brings us down to the responsibility these last two positions hold and why they are constant and visible. The apostle establishes the local church, the prophet guards and maintains the body of believers, and the evangelist protects and revives the vision of the body, while the pastor leads and the teacher instructs.

When we think of a pastor, we automatically think of a preacher who stands behind a pulpit and delivers a weekly message on Sunday. However, a pastor's responsibilities are more far reaching than just preaching. This is clearly established by the meaning of pastor—a shepherd.[1]

Spiritual shepherds are mentioned in both the Old and New Testaments, and both point to the one great shepherd of mankind, Jesus Christ. Psalm 23:1, Isaiah 40:11, and John 10 confirm that the Lord desires to be our shepherd. His heart and desire for His followers comprise a beautiful picture of the total abandonment and commitment of a shepherd towards the welfare of his sheep.

For example, a committed shepherd will not lead his sheep to muddy waters, to barren waste lands, or into danger. He does

---

[1] Strong's Exhaustive Concordance of the Bible, # 4166

44

everything to protect his sheep against predators, irritants such as fleas, and emotional stress such as fears. His goal is to bring his flock to still waters that revive, and green pastures that nourish.

This is a vision of a true shepherd. But today that vision is not prevalent. Many pastors in the Church appear as if they are failing to live up to this example. Some give the impression they have lost their heart or vision for shepherding. This makes a pastor a hireling shepherd or a self-centered wolf that is posing as a shepherd.

Shepherds who are void of heart and vision, lack the commitment to properly lead Jesus' sheep. Ezekiel 34 reveals the attitudes and works of both the hireling shepherds and those who are wolves among God's flock.

The first thing the prophet Ezekiel said about these shepherds is that they feed themselves rather than the sheep. We see this today as pastors or leaders are more interested in bigger buildings, kingdoms, and numbers, rather than individual sheep. Most of the pursuits of these worldly shepherds include money, prestige, and power instead of souls. Instead of leading the sheep to fresh water, they allow them to partake of muddy water (fleshly doctrine), stagnant water (dead-lettered doctrine), and poisoned water (blatant heresy). Instead of leading them to green pastures, they lead them to a spiritually barren wasteland where the sheep struggle to live, causing spiritual malnutrition, weakness, and death. Instead of protecting them, they allow the wolves to come in to devour the innocent lambs and to take down the vulnerable and wounded sheep. This is a classic example of the shepherds feeding their own self-serving purposes at the expense of the flock.

The second quality that Ezekiel brought out about a false shepherd is that he does not take care of the wounded sheep.[2] I have been in churches where the wounded fall through the cracks

---

[2] Ezekiel 34:4

of indifference, neglect, and statistics. In other words, the shepherd does not personally know the sheep. How can a pastor help a wounded soul unless he takes the time and energy to become personally involved with every individual who sits under their leadership?

This brings us to the mega-churches. They may appear impressive to the world and try to accommodate many people by having various pastors and programs. However, the wounded are being swallowed up by too much business that has been developed in the name of God. When you get right down to the operation of the church, it becomes obvious that it is a business venture.

This business is supposedly for the purpose of maintaining a religious kingdom. The meaning of Church has ceased to be that of a living body; rather, it has been rendered an unfeeling organization where many leaders' only goal is to see the masses flock in, instead of ensuring the individual is among the flock feeding on the Word of God.

Sadly, when the wounded sheep succumb to their open wounds and become missing, it goes unnoticed. Jesus said this in regard to the one missing sheep in Luke 15:4, "What man of you, having an hundred sheep, if he lose one of them, doth not leave the ninety and nine in the wilderness, and go after that which is lost, until he find it?"

One must keep in mind that a legitimate shepherd cares about every one of his sheep because he has personally invested in each one of them. Jesus is the one who purchased the sheep that sit in the church buildings throughout the world, not the earthly pastors. This is why souls are often treated as commodities by pastors. After all, what is one lost soul compared to the ninety-nine that are tithing, loyal, and visibly participating in the building of the pastor's personal kingdom?

46

Any time a pastor is without the heart of Jesus, they will lack the vision to see the worth of every soul who walks through the door of the church. I know that many pastors start out right, but with the worldly demands of maintaining physical growth and keeping up with the competition, the vision of souls can be choked out and lost among the various religious activities. Pastors must maintain the heart of Christ to ensure that the heavenly vision remains intact.

Because shepherds are neither properly feeding the real sheep of Jesus, nor having personal relationships with them, the sheep are being scattered as they search for personal leadership, pure water (the Word), and green pastures (nourishment). As the sheep scatter, they become prey to predators.

According to a figure I heard back in the 1980s, 80 percent of the kingdoms of the cults were made up of people who used to attend Christian churches. This simply means that the sheep looked elsewhere because the leadership or the body failed to do their part. Granted, some sheep are rebellious and will go their own way regardless of the investment, but the figure of 80 percent is an indictment against Christian leadership and the Body. Both have failed in some way, and both need to come back to Scripture and examine their attitudes, examples, and responsibilities to see where failure occurred.

Ezekiel 34:6 revealed where the failure occurred, "…and none did search or seek after them." Let me summarize the lacking ingredient that would produce such a response—the love of God.

Godly love is what causes one to make the proper investment in souls. This love compels a person to care for and seek after the one lost sheep. "Agape" love enables shepherds and believers to recognize and become identified with the wounded sheep, and it is this love that sets the Church apart from worldly indifference and self-serving kingdoms.

47

The love of God also produces a right attitude in the shepherd. A shepherd is also referred to as an elder, bishop, or overseer. Peter instructs these shepherds to feed the flock of God, not by harshness, but with a willing heart. They are not to feed them with financial gain in mind, but because they have the mind or determination to please the Shepherd that gave His life for the sheep. He also instructed them not to be superior in attitude, but an example of true leadership.[3] This leadership would come from an attitude of servitude, which expresses itself in meekness and lowliness.

This brings us down to the commission of the shepherd. It is quite simple. It is not to build big churches, establish great kingdoms, or have a great following. It is to simply feed God's sheep.

When Jesus told Peter that He would be part of the building of His Church, Peter probably envisioned great things for himself because of his pride. This pride set him up for great failure as he denied Jesus three times in the hour of his testing. The denial of Jesus put up a mirror that revealed Peter's depravity as his pride received a fatal blow.

When Jesus met with Peter after His resurrection, He asked Peter the same thing three times in order to rid Peter of misconceptions, allowing him to recognize his true responsibility. "Simon, son of Jonas lovest thou me more than these?" [4] I believe every true shepherd must go back to this simple question for, if the love is not there, they should step down from their position until the love once again abounds in their hearts. If they are representing Jesus without His heart of commitment, they are not only betraying their position and high calling, but they are betraying Jesus and His sheep.

---

[3] John 10:1-16; 1 Peter 5:1-4
[4] John 21:15-19

Once a shepherd can truly answer as Peter, "Yea Lord; thou knowest that I love thee," they will again grasp the importance of their position.[5] Once they properly perceive the motive behind their high calling, their commission will clearly be defined, their vision exalted to a heavenly perspective and hope, and their hearts in tune with the true Shepherd and Bishop of people's souls.[6] From this point, they will be able to hear the same instructions Jesus gave Peter—to feed His lambs, sheep, and flock.[7]

As I studied the writings and lives of the Apostle Paul and the Apostle Peter, I can see how their hearts and visions varied. They both established the Church, but Peter was a pastor and shepherd at heart. He understood the importance of this position like no other person in his situation, due to his experiences surrounding the cross and the calling of Jesus.

This is why Peter's warnings to pastors are as sobering as Ezekiel's. Ezekiel pronounced a "woe" on irresponsible shepherds and declared that God would seek His sheep and bind them up. He would also be against the false shepherds; and in due time He would take the flock away from them and feed the shepherds with judgment.[8]

Peter warned the shepherds who have been entrusted with Jesus' sheep to treat them properly, so that when the chief Shepherd appears, they would receive a crown of glory that would never fade.[9] Obviously, there will be some type of judgment rendered towards shepherds.

It amazes me that some pastors appear to be flippant about their positions. Many act as if their position is a profession or equivalent to the CEO of a big company. Instead of being a

---

[5] Ibid
[6] 1 Peter 2:25
[7] John 21:15-19
[8] Ezekiel 34:2, 10
[9] 1 Peter 5:1-4

humble servant to God's flock and a committed lover of Jesus Christ, such a pastor will have no problem merchandising souls and the things of God.

This reminds me of an incident with a pastor of a large church. He asked me what he needed to beware of in his position. I considered his responsibilities, staff, and grandiose goals. I looked at him and told him that his biggest challenge was not to leave his first love.[10]

It is easy to get caught up with good works and leave Jesus behind. Pastors have to guard their hearts and consider their ways to make sure they do not leave the source of their life, purpose, and strength behind. They must not forget that the sheep entrusted to them do not belong to them, and that, one day, they will give an account for the general spiritual condition of their flocks, as well as the sheep who are missing due to neglect, business, and worldliness on their parts.

I pray that every wayward pastor who has lost their vision will come back to the Chief Shepherd to renew and restore their life, calling, and commission. Restoration of the pastor's vision is necessary to prevent any further scattering of the sheep. A revived vision will allow the servant of God to be available to those sheep who are trying to find their way home. They will have the stamina to withstand the wolves, swine, and goats of their congregations, avoiding wounds and defeat. This vision will remind them to whom their allegiance must be directed towards, and what their responsibility is to Jesus' flock.

Teachers

The position of teacher in the Church is vital for edification. Without both the proper leadership of pastors and the instruction of teachers, the Church becomes subject to failure, destruction,

---

[10] Revelation 2:4

and death. Each of these five positions is vital to the complete edification of the Body, but pastors and teachers are the positions that ensure the growth and well-being of the Body. For example, apostles appeal to the spiritual needs of people, prophets appeal to the spiritual condition of people, and evangelists appeal to the vision of people, while shepherds appeal to the hearts of people and teachers appeal to the understanding of people. We see how all five positions result in what would be considered a complete picture of edification, but it is clear that pastors and teachers meet the Body at its point of personal needs and growth.

Teachers in Jesus' day were referred to as masters and rabbis. Another meaning for "teacher" was doctor.[11] The concept behind this position demanded respect from the pupils. But, the greatest reason for adhering to people placed in this position by God is because they directly influence a person's eternal destiny.

Today, the term teacher does not hold the same significance as it did in Jesus' day. In many cases, teaching is simply a position that needs to be filled, rather than a position that has been ordained by God. As we consider the idea of teaching in the kingdom of God, there are various goals to meet in order to ensure the integrity of this position.

Scriptural teaching points to discipline in every facet of life. It helps a person understand the path of righteousness, points them to walk in the ways of God's character, and instructs the individual in what it means to fear God and do His will.[12] Godly teaching is meant to get down into the spirit of man in order to change his perception, purpose, and direction.

Great teachers do not tell people how to think through indoctrination. Rather, they give them the tools that will challenge their ways of thinking. These teachers want to enlarge people's ability to consider the possibilities of a matter. It is not just a matter

---

[11] Strong's Exhaustive Concordance of the Bible, #1320
[12] Psalm 25:4, 8; 27:11; 143:10

of enlarging their ability to explore outside of the normal, intellectual boxes that many operate within, but it also is about enlarging one's world in regard to a matter.

Teaching in the kingdom of God must get down into a person's spirit to become life. For teaching to become a source of life and discovery, it must be manna from the throne room of God. This means it will be living, powerful, anointed, and inspired by the Holy Spirit. It will enable man to realize that spiritual truths cannot just be perceived as facts, intellectual conclusions, or doctrines. But they are to serve as milk, bread, meat, and life to the soul.

The real challenge for godly teachers is that they must do everything within their means to cause their students to exceed them in spiritual insight. In order to instruct students to come higher, these teachers must be experienced spiritual mountain climbers. They must know how to wisely enlarge their pupils enough that they can develop personal skills that will take them higher in Christ. After all, a teacher cannot lead students where they have never been, and students are only as good as their teacher.

Teachers shape minds by the type of emphasis or pursuits they uphold in their instructions. For example, my emphasis, as a servant of God, is a relationship with God. Valuable experiences have grown out of this pursuit. These experiences have given me authority in my teachings. Often, my emphasis will bring people back to this reality, but only the Spirit of God can impart it into a person's spirit to bring forth life.

The real authority and power of godly teachers becomes evident when they are serving as a conduit for the Holy Spirit to stir up the pupil with the anointed, pure Word of God. This will inspire the student to explore the possibilities of a greater reality of Christ. Such inspiration means the pupil's flame to discover truths beyond present understanding must be fanned into a fire.

This fire will cause them to pursue every bit of information presented, to reach and travel beyond present understanding.

Godly teachers encounter challenges because of how their students value or perceive truth. Students can fall into four categories. Some are like sponges. They soak everything up, but, because there is no commitment to comprehend the information in a personal way, they quickly dry out and change eludes them. Others are like the Dead Sea. They take much in, but the information never gets down to the heart to produce revelation and change. Then, you have those who take information in, but are like sieves. It all quickly flows through and out because there is no real foundation for any of it to rest upon.

The final group is made up of those who desire and seek after truth. They are not happy with facts, doctrine, or opinions. They want God's words to become life and substance to their souls. As a result, they see the Word as a gold mine and are forever seeking out nuggets that will make them grow in the knowledge of Jesus Christ.

Today, spiritual truths have been summarized into intellectual and doctrinal pursuits. People get excited about learning new facts and doctrines or confirming firmly held doctrines, but there seems no concern or desire to personally encounter Jesus in their pursuits.

I realize that students may not always give a good presentation of their teacher's commitment or emphasis, but, as a teacher, I want my students to have a basic understanding of godly principles. I realize that students determine how much depth of truth will reach into their souls and spirits. But every student still must understand basic foundational truths that will serve as a good foundation from which they have the abilities to explore the mysteries of God.

The question I must ask when I see Christians who lack this vital foundation is: What is their teacher's main emphasis? Paul warned of teachers who taught things that tickled fleshly ears, promoted the Law, and were a means to financial gain. Peter warned about teachers teaching damnable heresies, as well as people who would wrest Scriptures to their own destruction.[13] The warnings of false teachers and the destruction they wrought are manifold, but it is also clear about these imposters' final end—a greater condemnation.[14]

It is important, in each of the five positions, that the people who claim to hold them are actually called to them. They must be inspired and led by the Holy Spirit as they do the work of edification in the Body. As Ephesians 4:12-13 stated about the ultimate goal of these positions, "For the perfecting of the saints, for the work of the ministry, for the edifying of the body of Christ: Till we all come in the unity of the faith, and of the knowledge of the Son of God, unto a perfect man, unto the measure of the stature of the fullness of Christ." (Emphasis added)

These two Scripture verses tell us that servitude in God's kingdom is about perfecting saints so they can do the work of ministry for the building up of the Body. Godly edification produces unity in faith according to the knowledge of Christ. This type of edification causes a person to embrace the fullness of Christ so they can manifest Him to the Church and in the dark world.

Are you called to any of these positions? If so, are you being faithful to the leading of the Holy Spirit and the heart of Christ to bring people to spiritual maturity according to your calling and God's plan?

My main hope for all believers is that our Lord, Shepherd, and Savior will find the leadership in His Body faithful when He comes for His precious sheep.

---

[13] 1 Timothy 1:7; 4:1; 2 Timothy 4:3; Titus 1:11; 2 Peter 2:1; 3:18-16
[14] James 3:1

6

THE GIFTS OF GRACE

In Romans 12:6-8, we discover seven gifts that are to bring Christians to maturity. These gifts are not only for the edification of the Body, but they also are a means by which to reach out to the unsaved to touch their lives with the reality of Jesus. These gifts are given according to grace, and point to what some would consider natural abilities. However, God is the one who disperses them throughout the Body of believers.

To ensure these gifts are brought forth, the Apostle Paul set up the type of atmosphere that will allow them to manifest themselves in ministering the life of Christ to others. The first responsibility to secure and operate in these gifts is that a believer must present their body as a living sacrifice.[1]

The presentation of our bodies is for the purpose of consecration. Before consecration can take place, one must deny self, pick up the cross, and follow Jesus. Once the self-life is out of the way, a person can present their body to be set apart for God's use.

This separation allows the Holy Spirit to do the work of sanctification by transforming the mind of the person so that they can rightly discern what will be regarded as the good, acceptable, and perfect will of God. This transformed mind points to the mind

---

[1] Romans 12:1

of Christ. After all, He had one focus, purpose, and function—to do the will of the Father.[2]

The problem is that, until the mind is transformed, believers play guessing games as to what is pleasing to God. The usual test of such matters includes the following: 1) it has a religious tone to it; 2) it makes the individual feel good about self; and 3) it is a point of recognition of personal piousness.

Every blood-bought saint must have the same focus as Jesus in order to keep everything in perspective. As long as our minds are directed towards the so-called "goodness" of self, instead of the will of God, we will think more highly of ourselves than we ought to.[4]

Grace reminds us that we have no power to save ourselves; therefore, salvation was accomplished outside of any "personal goodness." We know this is true because Jesus secured our redemption on the cross. Our responsibility is to respond to this grace with the measure of faith allotted to us. This shows us that even the faith that we have available to properly respond to this work of grace comes from God.[5]

Grace is God's part in spiritual matters, but faith is man's response. Without the act of grace, man has no avenue by which to respond because he stands hopeless in his spiritual plight. Without faith responding to grace, God has no means by which to show His favor to a person. This is brought out in Romans 5:21, "That as sin hath reigned unto death, even so might grace reign through righteousness unto eternal life by Jesus Christ, our Lord." Faith is accounted to believers for righteousness when it comes to their state and actions as being righteous.[6] It is only at the point

---

[2] Philippians 2:5-11
[4] Romans 12:3
[5] Ibid
[6] Romans 4:3; 5:1-2

of righteousness that God's grace can reign in and through our lives.

Even the measure of faith is an act of grace. This measure of faith to respond properly to God's work and plan entails steps of obedience. As a person responds out of faith in obedience, the Holy Spirit meets the person in order to impart spiritual insight concerning the proper attitude toward and use of personal gifts for the glory of God and the edification of others.

Each time a person responds to the opportunity to exercise one of these gifts, they are enlarged in their faith to operate in the gift in greater measure. Such an attitude and approach point to being faithful before God concerning those things that He has entrusted to each of us. Christians who fail to be faithful with the gifts He has given them will not be entrusted with more, and their impact in lives will be non-existent or minimal.[7]

The atmosphere the Apostle Paul established in Romans 12 reveals that self must be out of the way to ensure that people will properly handle these gifts. Once the individuals are in the right disposition, God can effectively use them in any gift. These gifts are meant to be a natural extension of the working of His grace in their lives towards others. The purpose for these spiritual gifts is to bring Him glory.

I have broken these gifts down into two categories: gifts of servitude and gifts of benevolence. The reason for breaking down these gifts into two categories is because Jesus left us two distinct examples: servitude and suffering.[8] Once again, we are reminded that all true leaders in the kingdom of God are to be servants of all.

Keep in mind that godly leaders are defined by God's grace that should be displayed in them by the attitude of servitude. Therefore, grace will be evident in their actions and attitudes

---

[7] Luke 12:8; 16:10-12
[8] John 13:5-17; 1 Peter 2:19-25

towards those they are overseeing or ministering to. The four gifts that fall into the first category are prophecy, teaching, exhortation, and ruling.

Godly suffering occurs in two forms: persecution and entering into the sufferings with others. The second type of suffering is also known as compassion, which always produces benevolent acts. These acts are often sacrificial in nature as well as serve as a means of man extending grace to others in practical ways. The three gifts that fall into the second category are ministry, giving, and mercy.

It is important to point out that each of these gifts possess boundaries that bring discipline to them in order to ensure their proper use. Therefore, we must consider the gift in light of its discipline.

The first gifts we will consider are the gifts of servitude. These gifts find their authority and power within the attitude of servitude. Such gifts are brought under the leading of the Holy Spirit. Sensitivity to the Spirit results in a person showing discretion in regards to these gifts of grace. Without the right attitude and sensitivity, these gifts can become arrogant, hard, and indifferent.

The first gift in this category is prophecy. Prophecy has a couple of different meanings, but, since we are dealing with personal gifts, the correct meaning would imply an inspired speaker or preacher.

It is not enough to have the ability to be charismatic or to effectively speak or preach. For God to use any gift for His purpose, it must be prompted by the Holy Spirit. Therefore, prophecy, in this text, means an inspired speaker and preacher who only speaks according to the unction of the Holy Spirit. This would mean that the speaker would be imparting living manna from the throne of God.

Inspirational speaking of this caliber manifests authority, boldness, and power. It will penetrate the souls of man, "...piercing even to the dividing asunder of soul and spirit, and of the joints and marrow, and is a discerner of the thoughts and intents of the heart," powerfully impacting the hearers" (Hebrews 4:12). We can witness this natural ability to pierce and separate in action through Spirit-led pastors and evangelists.

The boundary or discipline of the gift of prophecy is that it must be done according to the proportion of faith. The hearers, not the preacher, will determine the proportion of faith in which this gift is exercised. For example, a preacher who is being led by the Spirit will have a sense of where their hearers are spiritually. This will dictate the emphasis of the person's message.

The next gift is teaching. This gift is self-explanatory, but, once again, a teacher must wait before God as to the type of manna that must be offered to the hearers. The purpose of teaching is to instruct others, but the boundary of this gift implies that it goes beyond just instructing others. The goal of teaching, in this text, points to providing the necessary tools to the recipients so they can, in turn, instruct others.

Good teachers inspire curiosity to explore beyond comfortable truths and doctrines. Committed teachers want to see their students exceed their instructions and reach greater heights of understanding and maturity. Sadly, much of teaching simply deals with the facts. Believers are busy feeding their minds with facts. As a result, many people become like the Dead Sea. Information is poured into them, but it is never imparted elsewhere, resulting in spiritual stagnation.

Every Christian should be quick to instruct, whether it is through teaching, sharing, or being a visible example of God's grace and love. The problem is that much of what believers understand is not living, which means there is no heavenly vision and inspiration behind it.

Teaching which lacks heavenly vision and inspiration will lack the power to impact lives and bring forth changes. After all, powerful teachings not only stir up curiosity, but they challenge intellectual comfort zones, spiritual complacency, and personal piousness.

According to *Strong's Concordance,* "exhortation" means to call near, invite, invoke, implore, console, comfort, desire, interact, and pray. This definition not only shows servitude, but benevolence. Those who exhort will preach the Gospel, invite people to fellowship with God through Jesus, and invoke them to be holy and upright. An exhorter will implore people to repent of their sins, console those who are suffering, and comfort those who are sorrowful.

The desire of godly exhortation is to see people love, serve, and follow Jesus. This means exhorters must interact with people in meekness and humility, as well as earnestly intercede in prayer for them.

When you combine all of these ingredients of exhortation, you have an individual who will, "contend for the faith which was once delivered unto the saints" (Jude 3). To contend or wrestle for the faith of others can be an intense, thankless, and drawn-out process. This is why those with the gift of exhortation need to keep eternity in focus to maintain a right attitude and perspective.

However, it is vital that those with the gift of exhortation wait for the Spirit's leading. They must show discretion. The hearer must be prepared, as well as the one who is exhorting. The goal of exhortation is to prepare others to contend for the faith. The Church needs leaders who will have compassion on Jesus' sheep, but will also contend with sheep who are erring with the intent to pull them out of the fire of destruction.[9]

The final gift in the category of servitude is the ruler. To be a ruler means to preside, practice, maintain, or be over. It points to someone who can be an effective administrator.[10]

[9] James 5:19-20; Jude 22-23
[10] Strong's Exhaustive Concordance, # 4291

This individual has the natural abilities to lead. However, to be an effective leader in the kingdom of God, they must know how to follow. A ruler who is not submissive, teachable, and humble will not be a powerful leader in God's kingdom. A leader who has not truly been humbled by the Lordship of Jesus is not open to instruction and will lack healthy fear to keep this position in proper perspective.

Real leaders in the kingdom of God lead more by example than words. This is why they must have the attitude of a servant and the actions of a trustworthy leader who is truly representative of Jesus Christ.

The boundary established for the ruler in God's kingdom is that they must rule with diligence. According to *Strong's Concordance*, "diligence" means speed, dispatched, earnest, and eager. Godly leaders must be speedy in seeking God's wisdom in confronting problems that affect the local body. They must be able to wisely disperse responsibilities to others to bring about spiritual growth and be quick to stop discord or destruction among Christians. They must be earnest about their responsibilities and eager to serve as God's mouth, heart, hands, and feet. They must practice meekness and maintain purity of heart and leadership in all spiritual matters.

Now that we have looked at the gifts of servitude, ask the Lord which gift or gifts He has entrusted to you. Once your gift or gifts are established, ask Him to give you grace to display the attitude of a student, the example of a follower of Jesus, and the ability to properly use these abilities. Keep in mind that these gifts are meant to edify each member of the body, to become living witnesses to those who are perishing and to bring glory to God.

7

GIFTS OF BENEVOLENCE

At the heart of God is benevolence. Due to His great act of benevolence displayed on the cross for each of us, the Lord expects His people to display the same attitude that will produce sacrificial actions.

Benevolence is as much of an attitude as it is an action. The attitude that is expressed most in benevolence is selflessness. This is important because real benevolence is going to sacrificially cost something. If an individual is indifferent or self-serving, they will always fall short of showing true benevolence.

This is obvious when you consider that the greatest act of benevolence in the history of man came from Jesus. He gave up the glories of heaven, became both servant and man to become identified with humanity. He walked among people to personally touch them. He entered in at every point of human suffering to minister to hurting and lost souls. He made the ultimate sacrifice to redeem mankind. He clearly defined benevolence through His acts of kindness. His actions revealed that our good will was at the heart of His attitude and service.

The motivation behind benevolence is love. This love is not an emotional love that shows sympathy. Sympathy is superficial and lasts only as long as the emotion. Such an emotion is self-serving and always causes the sympathizer to feel good about self. It prides itself in its emotional involvement, but lacks both substance and action. It claims the glory without paying the price.

Benevolence is empathy. This means a person will actually enter in with the individual at the point of their plight. It is selfless because it is compelled by the sacrificial love of God to take moral responsibility for the welfare of others. It is not conscious of its actions or sacrifices; therefore, its kindness is natural, unconditional, and generous. It is not seeking to receive personal rewards, nor is it after personal glory or recognition because it is devoid of selfish motives and personal agendas. A good example of this benevolence is found in the actions of the Good Samaritan in Luke 10.

True benevolence will test the character of a person. Many people think they are benevolent when, in reality, they fail the test of benevolence when they are required to go the extra mile. They give up before they pay the ultimate price or finish the course. They stop at a few good acts by convincing themselves they did their part. They become agitated if a person's needs supersede their "good-will". They become angry when they don't get the desired response from their actions.

Benevolence is not a feeling or an emotion that has been stirred up by some emotional ploy. It is a commitment that is ready to act with sensitivity. It is quick to recognize the plight of others because the heart is tender, open, and available to enter in with people in practical ways. In fact, the earmark of Christianity is benevolence.

It is genuine benevolence that sets the real Church apart and attracts people to the kingdom of God. Sadly, this virtue is missing. Christians in America appear to have lost sight of what constitutes benevolence. They give enough to soothe their religious conscience, while they heap the things of the world upon themselves. Some give to get back, while others give to impersonal organizations to avoid personal involvement with needy people. Yet, God calls His people to become personally identified with others in their plights to ensure blessings and avoid judgment and spiritual poverty.

It is important to point out that blessings are not the same as spiritual treasures and riches. Blessings often have to do with the outer man and point to worldly riches, while spiritual treasures have to do with the inward man and the unseen riches of heaven. The Apostle Paul reveals that Jesus Christ is the real treasure of the Christian. Therefore, a person's riches come down to how much of Christ they possess.[1]

Most people prefer blessings that will personally minister to the outer man, but fail to consider treasure that will not rot, but will ensure godly character, substance, and satisfaction to the inner man. We get a glimpse of this in Hebrews 11 where it talks about people experiencing blessings as they subdued kingdoms, obtained promises, escaped the edge of the sword, and received their dead, but, "others were tortured, not accepting deliverance that they might obtain a better resurrection" (Hebrews 11:35). The latter group was denying physical blessings in order to pursue heavenly treasure.

This is why the Apostle Paul instructed Christians to set their affections on things above.[2] If believers are seeking after heavenly treasures, they will not be part of the "bless me" club of America. Ultimately, they will become more caught up with Jesus than with the world.

Due to the emphasis on worldly blessings, many American Christians appear as if they are preparing to stay here on earth, rather than abide forever with Jesus. Instead of being sojourners, many have put roots down in this world that will prove to be devoid of benevolence.

---

[1] Philippians 3:10-14; Colossians 2:2-3
[2] Colossians 3:2

Godly-inspired benevolence has a touch of heaven and is beyond this world's comprehension. All benevolent deeds are acts as well as gifts of grace that point to the example of Jesus Christ. This is why this virtue will go the extra mile without complaining, give without expecting anything in return, and go on to the next opportunity of service without remembering the deeds of yesterday.

It is important to realize that, without the touch and reality of heaven, people with these gifts will not be able to fully operate in them. They will fall short along the way. This is why we must remember that these seven gifts are an act of grace from God. Therefore, they must find their real source in God's love and their real inspiration and power in submission to the work of the Holy Spirit.

This brings us to the last three gifts of grace. The number "three" represents entirety or completeness. In these last gifts, we can see the position and attitude behind true benevolence and how it points to the effective ministry of Jesus Christ as the Servant to servants.

The gift of ministry points to position. According to *Srong's Concordance,* this word means one who attends, aids, offers official service, and brings relief. Another word for minister is "deacon." Therefore, ministry points to a true servant who is ready to attend any need, aid in any project, and offer any point of service where needed, and who will ultimately bring much needed relief.

This is why the Bible refers to believers or saints as ministers. Our whole mission in life is to learn to minister in order to inspire reconciliation. But this reconciliation cannot take place unless ministry has a touch from heaven. It must be done in much patience, affliction, necessity, and distress.[3] People must see that

---

[3] 2 Corinthians 3:6; 5:18: 6:4

godly ministry goes beyond good deeds to embrace gentleness. It speaks of a sacrifice that is supernatural in nature.

As believers, we must learn such ministry at the feet of Jesus. Very few people learn to wait at His feet while the Lord ministers to them. They miss the satisfaction that comes from abiding in Him. After all, Jesus is our Vine and we must not move until He does. This example shows us that Jesus is not after ministry, but after our hearts, attention, and senses.

In Luke 10:38-42, we see Martha serving Jesus, while Mary sat at His feet. From all appearances, Martha was proving her worth, while Mary was selfishly enjoying the presence of Jesus. When Martha became upset over Mary's apparent lack of service, she pointed it out to Jesus. Jesus' words would have seemed strange if you didn't understand the importance of waiting before Him, "Martha, Martha, thou are careful and troubled about many things: But one thing is needful: and Mary hath chosen that good part, which shall not be taken away from her."

As you can see, the boundary for ministry is to wait for the expected time. Waiting prepares people for God's appointed time and purpose. It is a way of renewing the strength so a person can go the extra distance, reviving the vision so they can effectively count the cost, and being given the power to finish the course for the glory of God.[4]

Since Mary took the time to sit at the feet of Jesus, she, in turn, had been prepared to minister to Jesus at a very important time in His life. We see this incident in John 12:3-7. Mary was the one who anointed Jesus ahead of time for His burial. This ointment was very costly to Mary, but she humbly offered it to Him as she anointed His feet with it and then wiped His feet with her hair. The smell of this ointment not only filled the room, but also reached the

---

[4] Isaiah 40:31

throne room of God. Her very act now serves as a memorial to others.[5]

The key to the length of waiting must rest solely with the presence of God and the leading of His Spirit. If His presence is present, a minister must sit in preparation and expectation and wait until the Holy Spirit moves. We see this same scenario with the Israelites. They only moved when the cloud moved and waited when the cloud abided in their midst.[6]

The effectiveness of a minister will be determined by how much they learn the lesson of waiting in expectation for the time when God calls them forth to do His bidding.

This brings us to the second gift of benevolence. The virtue that is consistent in this second gift is giving. Righteous giving is ready to give out of its needs, share what it has without reservation, and impart without conditions. This shows that giving is generous in nature.

We see this generosity in Israel. A call went out to the children of Israel to willingly bring God an offering to establish the tabernacle, a dwelling place for Him.[7] According to Exodus 36:3-7, the children of Israel brought so many offerings that they had to be constrained to stop. The problem today is that much of the Church must be compelled to give, and it is usually done by emotional manipulation. This type of giving lacks genuine commitment, making it temporary and conditional.

The reason that the people of Israel freely gave was because they realized God had given them everything they possessed. After all, they were former slaves in Egypt; therefore, they were glad to adhere to God's call.

The problem with some of the Church is that its vision is not eternal and its hearing has become dulled by fleshly and worldly

---

[5] Leviticus 2:2, 9, 16; 2 Corinthians 2:15-16; Matthew 26:12-13
[6] Exodus 13:21-22
[7] Exodus 25:1 & 2

pursuits. Giving has ceased to be a valuable calling of the whole Body, in spite of the fact that every possession comes from God. For the Body of Christ, the act of giving should be a natural response to show appreciation towards God, who has given His Church everything. This type of benevolence shows reliance on God to continue to give according to people's needs and His eternal plan.

We can see this total reliance on God with the widow and her mites. She gave it all to God, showing faith in God to be her provider. Jesus actually pointed her out as giving more than all who gave that day because, "...they did cast in of their abundance, but she of her want did cast in all that she had even all her living" (Mark 12:44)

The widow gave all back to God and now serves as our example to true, acceptable giving. This proves that acceptable giving will actually cost the individual in such a way that it ultimately makes the person needy and dependent towards God. Giving of this nature is done in faith, but it is this type of giving that God can honor and multiply. It is in the multiplication that we see the touch of heaven.

We see this multiplication factor in the feeding of the five thousand in John 6. Jesus could have made stones into bread, but, instead, He took a lunch of a young boy and multiplied it. Consider this boy's situation.

It happened to be his lunch, yet he gave it up. As a result, Jesus fed thousands with it. This clearly shows us that God wants to be a co-laborer with us in this harvest field, but we first must faithfully offer everything back to Him that He has entrusted to us.

The reason so much eludes the American Church today is because many will not trust God with that which He has entrusted to them. They hoard temporary goods to ensure an uncertain future and heap upon themselves the things of life, only to experience the vanity of the world. Even though they have been entrusted with much, they will give very little to God. As a result, He cannot multiply it in order to impact others in a powerful way.

The boundary for the gift of giving is simplicity. Simplicity points to giving that is not self-serving, but is pure, faithful, and liberal. This shows that acceptable giving must be done with the right motive—to impact others with the intention of bringing glory to God.

The main purpose of giving must be to bring glory to God. This motive will allow His followers to get beyond earthly concerns and be generous about eternal matters that will exalt and honor the Lord.

Giving is at the heart of God's love. As Jesus pointed out with the widow and her mites, it is not what we give that shows our devotion, but what we give out of our own personal need. We see this very attitude in the new Church in Acts 2:44 and 4:32-37.

The new Church was so giving that there were none among them who lacked. Some sold houses and lands to ensure the Body was properly taken care of. Is it any wonder that many were added to the Church by such examples of benevolence?

We can never out give God, but are we willing to give above the required, acceptable, or normal idea of giving? Are we willing to give in such a way that the world could actually see a contrast as God multiplied it for His glory?

Much of the Church lacks the benevolence that comes out of the love of God, but those who have a gift of giving must understand how it works. It will mean nothing unless all is generously offered to God, so He can touch it for His work and glory.

Those with this gift must realize that they are to serve as conduits for the Holy Spirit to distribute God's goodness to others through faithful, sacrificial giving. This type of giving is distinct because it will speak of something beyond this world that is powerful and life changing.

The keys to this giving are the love of God, the power of the Spirit, and faithfulness to the blessings, gifts, and means that God has provided, regardless of how small or great.

The final gift in this category is mercy. Lamentations 3:22-23 states, "It is of the LORD'S mercies that we are not consumed because his compassions fail not. They are new every morning: great is thy faithfulness." Mercy points to the act of restraint from judgment that produces compassion. Compassion is the ability to enter in, which actually is the truest form of grace in action.

Jesus showed us this mercy when He took on the form of a servant and was fashioned as a man. He was tempted in all areas and tasted the harshness of life, the hatred of man, and the darkness of death.

He entered into people's plights such as the woman at the well, the woman caught in idolatry, and Zacchaeus. He touched lives, thereby, changing these people's plight and often their eternal destination. He still impacts the world today as the High Priest. As man, He understands the temptation and struggles that often besets man, but, as God, He knows the heart of God. Because of this combination, He is able to bring both together into reconciliation.[8]

As our High Priest, Jesus' intercession still gives us glimpses into how this mercy still works on our behalf before the throne of God. It is beyond human means because in our humanity we are unable to turn the other cheek in humiliation or persecution, unless self is out of the way and the Spirit of God is serving as our strength. Mercy cannot go the extra mile unless compelled to do so by the love of God.

Mercy without the power of the Holy Spirit turns into sympathy and, without the love of God as the motive, it turns into self-pity. Ultimately, sympathy produces self-righteousness that will judge,

---

[8] 2 Corinthians 5:18-20; 1 Timothy 2:5

while self-pity makes a person into an insipid martyr who justifies sin, anger, and resentment.

God's mercy does not consider offenses, for His love covers a multitude of sins, and His compassions never fail. His heart is the same towards all as He seeks out the one lost sheep.[9]

This is the face of mercy. It is truly a gift from heaven because man is devoid of any personal virtue that comes close to this gift. Granted, people often have high opinions about their love and hospitality. But, when tested, these characteristically lack the heavenly touch, perseverance, and sacrifice that are so prevalent in the gift of mercy.

Mercy that does not have the right spirit and motive of love behind it will prove to be destructive. Proverbs 12:10 states, "A righteous man regardeth the life of his beast: but the tender mercies of the wicked are cruel."

Mercy is a discipline that restrains the person from executing any type of judgment. According to James 2:12-13 when applied to judgment true mercy is capable of pardoning the offender when they seek it. Judgment, on the other hand, can only separate the offender to pay the necessary consequences.

For mercy to win, one must have the right attitude, spirit, and motive to walk in it as well as execute it in place of judgment. Consider the necessary ingredients to ensure real mercy is in operation when it comes to ministry towards others:

Mercy without grace becomes conditional and cruel.

Mercy without compassion becomes indifferent.

Mercy without patience become judgmental.

Mercy without love becomes impatient and accusing.

This may explain why the boundary of this gift of mercy is cheerfulness. Cheerfulness, in this text, is a willingness to go the extra distance. It is prompted by undivided devotion, not

---

[9] Luke 15:1-10; 1 Peter 4:8

begrudging about costly sacrifice and is overjoyed when it comes to giving all for the glory of God.

The gifts of benevolence are indeed a picture of God's sacrificial love coming forth through grace. His grace serves as an extended helping hand towards those who are lost, weary, alone, and afraid.

Ask the Lord what benevolent gifts He has entrusted to you. Once He reveals what the gift or gifts may be, ask Him to give you the love, heavenly vision, and grace to properly operate in the gift or gifts for His glory.

8

SUPERNATURAL GIFTS

The next categories of gifts that will be discussed create the most controversy. This controversy has not only nullified the part these gifts play in spiritual maturity, but it has undermined the concept of edification.

The Holy Spirit, not the will of man, controls these gifts. This means they are supernatural in nature and are given according to the will of the Spirit.

Many are aware of the debate that argues whether or not these gifts ceased after the initial birth and growth of the new Church. This argument is based on 1 Corinthians 13:8-10. These Scriptures are interpreted as saying that the gifts of the Holy Spirit were done away with because perfection had arrived; therefore, there was no longer any need for them. I could agree with this conclusion except it does not remain consistent with the work and purpose of the Spirit that has been clearly displayed throughout the complete counsel of God.

There are a couple of important points we must look at according to the intent behind the instruction concerning these gifts, and not according to the intellectual evaluation of man that is limited, denominational, and often biased. The Apostle Paul is clear to point out that man only knows in part. If you study the nine gifts of the Spirit, you will see that they actually are designed to bring understanding where man's inability and frailties keep him from seeing beyond the flesh into the spiritual realm. These gifts operate on a temporary basis for they only come as the Spirit wills.[1] In other words, they are not constant or always present like the gifts of grace that are found in Romans 12.

These supernatural gifts work beyond man's limited knowledge and not only open him up to the supernatural, but also reveal the heart and mind of God. Even though Scripture points out that man sees through a glass darkly, he often believes he understands all he needs to grasp in order to arrive at a right conclusion. After all, he has looked at all the angles, logically thought it out in his mind, and found the Scriptures to confirm his conclusions. But, as the Apostle Paul echoed in Scripture, "man knows only in part."[2] Therefore, spiritual gifts that cannot be controlled by man are given not only to show that man can only see in part, but also to show that his reliance must be on the Holy Spirit to effectively minister to others in the Church.

The second point we must examine in light of this debate is what constitutes perfection. Apparently, these gifts will be in operation until that which is perfect comes. For these gifts to cease early in the Church age would mean that the appointed perfection came into the midst of the early Church and completed its work. But what work is that? The Church has not reached a state of perfection; therefore, what could be considered perfect?

Some believe that the Word of God represents that perfection, but there is nowhere in Scripture that such a theory is verified. Scripture clearly states that the work of perfection for the Church will continue until the coming of Jesus Christ. We know scripturally that the only person or source that is considered perfect is the Person of Jesus Christ.[3]

---

[1] 1 Corinthians 12:11
[2] 1 Corinthians 13:9, 12
[3] Philippians 1:6

Jesus has not come, and it is clear that the Church is operating in a limited fashion in spite of the intellectual or doctrinal resources that might be available to it. Therefore, one must conclude that the gifts are still in operation and available to help edify believers in their imperfection and limitations. In fact, the Church will be in the stage of being brought to perfection or maturity until the Bridegroom comes for her.

Due to the controversy over these supernatural gifts, the Holy Spirit has been quenched or grieved in this area. Since part of the development of the Church involves the correct application of gifts for the benefit or profit of the whole Body, this living organism has greatly suffered.[4]

The Apostle Paul made it clear in his epistles that the leadership positions and gifts were for the main purpose of making the Church into a fine-tuned body that works in harmony.[5] He called for all of the members of this Body to be servants, and to have unity according to godly love, a right foundation, and a right spirit.

In order to bring forth this harmony, there is only one Spirit who distributes the diverse gifts among the different members of the Body for its growth. There is also one Lord who oversees the different aspects of ministries within the Church to ensure order; and there is only one God who knows how to work maturity through these various operations into the soul of the Body.[6]

This formidable leadership of the Godhead over the Church is to ensure the Body operates according to Spirit and truth and not the flesh. The positions and gifts have a spiritual nature to them that are capable of bringing believers higher in their relationships with God and empowering the Church with authority to carry out

[4] 1 Corinthians 12:7
[5] Romans 12:3-8; Ephesians 4:4-16
[6] 1 Corinthians 12:4-6

its commission. It also has a heavenly vision to walk in confidence and the strength to stand as the salt and light in this dark world.

Sadly, the Church's prideful debate over this subject has demoted the gifts to a fleshly arena. They have been placed in Satan's camp by ignorance, fear, or ungodly exaltation that discredits and often mocks their purpose in the Body.

Once again, we must remind ourselves of the instructions found In Ephesians 4:4-16. We are told that the Church was given the necessary tools for the purpose of edifying or building this Body up into a healthy representation of Jesus Christ. Every position and gift have one purpose and goal in mind. That goal is to bring the whole Body together "in the unity of the faith, and the knowledge of the Son of God, unto a perfect man unto the measure of the stature of the fullness of Christ" (Ephesians 4:13).

After studying the attitude and status of the modern Church, it is apparent that many of its members have lost sight of the spiritual birth, nature, and function of the Body. They have reduced the Church into a worldly organization that is bound by denomination and not the love of God. Much of this Body puts faith in their intellectual understanding and interpretation of Scripture, rather than allowing the Spirit of the Living God, to lead them into all truth.[7]

It is time to get rid of our intellectual interpretation of the Word and come back to square A. The truth is the new struggling Church of the first three centuries after Christ's ascension proved to be powerful because Scripture was not a matter of doctrinal interpretation, but of truths that needed to be upheld in spirit and practical obedience.

As I compare the spiritual condition of the young, New Testament Church to our modern-day Church, especially in places such as America where worldly abundance and self-sufficiency

---

[7] John 16:13

have been in operation, I can see a diverse difference. Much of the visible Church of today, with its entire intellectual prowess, is weak, worldly, and ineffective.

As part of this Body, I have come to recognize that all of our pursuit for truths according to higher learning and denominational influences has made us expert debaters of the Word rather than lovers of it. We are not richer for our theological understandings and differences. We are poorer for them. In fact, we are missing the simplicity behind the order and function of the Body of Christ. Unlike the young Church, many in the modern-day Church would not be able to stand. They do not know how to hear the voice of God and adhere to the Holy Spirit's leading. As a result, it appears as if much of the present-day Body has closed down the avenues in which the Holy Spirit operates.

In the Church's attempt to fit all beliefs into personal comfort zones and denominational preferences, it has succumbed to unbelief as its different members pick and choose to interpret certain areas of the Bible away with higher education or denominational creeds. Not only have many in the Church ceased to believe the truths of the Bible, but many have also become religious fools and scoffers of those truths that do not fit into their nice little doctrinal boxes. In such unbelief, people develop hard hearts as their ways of religion ultimately become empty and useless to them in a world designed to exalt man and his knowledge over the so-called "fables" of the Bible.[8]

Much of the visible Church in America must come back to center because it has lost its way. It is no better for its endless education or theological debates. It is not more powerful because of its divisions or more respected because of its incessant demand of being right about certain spiritual matters.

The Church needs to cease being a parasite that feeds on the pride or ignorance of others to prove a senseless spiritual point.

---

[8] Hebrews 3:7-19

Rather, it needs to regain the heavenly vision of how each member is meant to function for the benefit of the whole Body for the glory of God.

I have often wondered what the Apostle Paul would say about the Church in America. Would he accuse the Church of being bewitched like the Galatians, carnal like the Corinthians, or unrealistic like the Thessalonians? Would he compare much of the Body to the church of Ephesus that had much work, but no love? Maybe he would show the Body that most of it possesses wrong doctrine like Pergamum, is committing spiritual harlotry like Thyatira, is dead like Sardis, or lukewarm like Laodicea.

On the other hand, how would our present-day religious leaders respond to the Apostle Paul if he confronted them? Would he be able to commend some, while rebuking many others?

What is your attitude towards the supernatural gifts? Have you closed down this spiritual avenue because of theology? Are you confused because of the debate over it? Are you open to these gifts, even though you don't understand them, or is your understanding of them correct?

I believe this issue has to be resolved because the Church in America is coming into a time of great spiritual darkness and all of our theology, denominational beliefs, and spiritual knowledge will not prepare or enable us to withstand it. Only the Holy Spirit will be able to instruct, warn, and lead us through it. But, how many of us are prepared to hear what the Spirit is truly saying in these days?[9]

---

[9] John 16:13c

9

DIVERSITY OF GIFTS

While studying the supernatural gifts in 1 Corinthians 12 and 14, I recognized the working of the Godhead in the function of both the Body and the gifts. When considering the Body, the Holy Spirit baptizes each member into it. The Body is being molded into the image of the Son and will serve as His extension in this lost world. Based on God the Father's design and plan, each member is set into the Body, with the intent of tempering this living organism together. This work of the Godhead is to ensure edification and unification of the whole Body.[1]

We see the Godhead working within the area of gifts as well. As we will see, the Lord administers these gifts to ensure order in the Body and the Father determines how they will operate in the Body to ensure their integrity. However, it is the Spirit who distributes the gifts. These different gifts actually serve as a manifestation of the Holy Spirit in the Body.[2]

There are nine supernatural gifts. It has been interesting to observe the numbers used in positions and gifts. These numbers show the consistent order and work of God. Remember that there are five positions that point to grace, seven gifts of grace that symbolize perfection, and now we have nine supernatural gifts. The number "nine" points to the work of the Holy Spirit. We see

---

[1] 1 Corinthians 12:12-13, 18, 24, 27
[2] 1 Corinthians 12:4, 7

this number in the fruit of the Spirit.[3] Nine also is a number of "finality." The Holy Spirit's work is complete and will bring forth perfection or maturity.

The Holy Spirit is the one who gives these gifts according to His will for the profit of man and the Church.[4] In fact, man has nothing to do with these gifts except to allow the Holy Spirit to use him as a vessel in which to express Himself.

Once again, we are reminded that there are differences of administrations, but the same Lord. Administration points to aid, service, or servant.[5] These gifts are to aid or serve the Body in accordance with the attitude and example of the Son of God, who is not only the head of the Body, but is Lord over it. As Jesus said, "If I then, your Lord and Master, have washed your feet; ye also ought to wash one another's feet. For I have given you an example, that ye should do as I have done to you" (John 13:14-15).

1 Corinthians 12:6 told us there are also diversities of operations, but it is the same God who works all in all. This refers to God the Father. (See 1 Corinthians 8:6.) Philippians 1:6 states, "Being confident of this very thing, that he which hath begun a good work in you will perform it until the day of Jesus Christ."

Diversity of operations points to effect, power, and work. God the Father wants to produce a certain effect with these gifts. In order to do this, the power must be available to work this effect or result within the body. This effect will not only be in accordance with His will and eternal plan, but it will bring Him glory.

These three divisions of gifts show that there are three main purposes behind these gifts that will result in edification. They will serve as an expression of the Spirit, honor the leadership of Jesus, and glorify the Father.

---

[3] Galatians 5:22-23
[4] 1 Corinthians 12:7, 11
[5] 1 Corinthians 12:5

The number "three" points to the Godhead and completeness. We can begin to see that the gifts are not only meant to edify, but to unify the Body and make it complete. After all, without the presence and power of the Spirit, the leadership of Jesus, and the work of the Father according to His perfect design, there is no completion. The Body would be nothing more than an empty shell.[6]

Another number three can be found in the division of the nine gifts. Harold Horton, in his book entitled *The Gifts of the Spirit,* broke these gifts down into three categories.[7] They are gifts of revelation, gifts of power, and gifts of inspiration.

The gifts of revelation point to those areas of truths, problems, or sins that must be supernaturally uncovered by the Holy Spirit. His purpose for using these gifts is to bring to light hindrances, struggles, or works of darkness in order to instruct, exhort, encourage, or warn. These gifts become the means by which to express not only God's awareness of a person's spiritual condition or plight, but also His infinite insight into all matters. Although, at times, people may convince themselves that He does not know or really care about them, nothing is hidden from our omniscient God. He uses these gifts to bring this reality to the forefront. The gifts that fall into the category of revelation are word of wisdom, word of knowledge, and discerning of spirits.

The gifts of power involve the supernatural intervention of God. In these gifts, God's power is often displayed in a miraculous way. However, these gifts work within two boundaries: man's faith and God's sovereign will. They are often used for confirmation or to bring glory to God. Gifts that fall into this category are faith, healing, and miracles.

The gifts of inspiration are considered the vocal gifts and are used as a means for God to be heard. They are the gifts of

---

[6] See Ezekiel 37:1-10
[7] © 1934

prophecy, tongues, and interpretation of tongues. The Holy Spirit must inspire the vessel or person to speak forth what He gives them, but the vessel must willfully submit as the instrument.

Inspirational gifts usually occur during worship when God's people are praising Him. After all, He inhabits the praises of His people.[8] These gifts also have strict guidelines set down in 1 Corinthians 14 to prevent chaos and confusion. Chaos and confusion occur when these gifts are being improperly used or abused for personal vainglory or spiritualism.

By keeping in mind, the different functions of these gifts, one will be more realistic about them, instead of fearful and superstitious. Each of these gifts is God's means of working within the Body and is beyond or outside of man's realm. They are clearly supernatural and are meant to bring the awe of God and awareness of His commitment back into the midst of man.

Sadly, the gifts of inspiration have caused the great controversy that has resulted in many ignoring or abusing these gifts. As a result, these nine supernatural gifts have been brought down into the arena of unbelief and debates, discrediting or closing down this vital avenue of edification.

Consider your attitude towards these gifts. Are you open or closed to them? Are you ignorant about them, or do you show prejudicial opposition when confronted with their use? Make sure your attitudes line up with the Word of God and not denominational preference and indoctrination.

---

[8] Psalm 22:3

10

WORD OF WISDOM

Before we can consider the gift of wisdom, we must have a proper perspective about godly wisdom. James 3:17 states, "But the wisdom that is above is first pure, then peaceable, gentle, and easy to be intreated, full of mercy and good fruits, without partiality and without hypocrisy." All godly wisdom comes from God and manifests itself in godliness. Its goal is to obtain peace with God, be gentle in response, and be quick to listen and learn. It is full of mercy that results in compassion and forgiveness. It is neither biased nor insincere.

Godly wisdom has a touch of heaven that is simple in presentation. This wisdom is developed as a person submits to God and becomes obedient to His ways and Word. It is fine-tuned as righteousness wins over temptation, arrogance gives way to humility, conceit yields to godly instruction, foolishness submits to sobriety, and knowledge is applied in godly ways.[1]

This wisdom is founded on the fear of God; therefore, its warnings are heeded and its instructions obeyed. It has the power to deliver because it teaches discretion and makes one vigilant. It rewards because it enables a person to walk in liberty, to embrace life, and to discover its treasures.

This wisdom can be summarized in two words—Jesus Christ. "But of him are ye in Christ Jesus: who of God is made unto us

---

[1] Proverbs 1

wisdom..." (1 Corinthians 1:30). Wisdom will be manifested in a person's life through the manifestation of Jesus Christ. His very nature expounds wisdom and expresses itself through His attitude and responses towards others.

God's wisdom is quite different from man's wisdom. James 3:14-16 describes the wisdom of man,

> But if ye have bitter envying and strife in your hearts, glory not, and lie not against the truth. This wisdom descendeth not from above, but is earthly, sensual, devilish. For where envying and strife are, there is confusion and every evil work.

We can see man's wisdom is self-serving and competitive. It will produce jealousy and strife when it finds itself being challenged or not properly recognized. It often walks in confusion because it is hypocritical and unrealistic. This wisdom is not only earthly and sensual, but will display a demonic influence that will complicate, pervert, and defile truth.

Godly wisdom is often established or developed through obedience. However, the wisdom that is given by the Holy Spirit for the purpose of edification is a gift that is meant to address a particular situation in the life of an individual or in the conduct of the Body. This gift can edify a person to whom it is directed, but it has the capacity of edifying the whole body because it always has a point of godly instruction.

The word of wisdom actually gives insight into the mysteries and mind of God concerning a matter. It not only serves as a point of instruction, but can also be a means of encouraging, exhorting, or warning. Ultimately, it will line up to God's character and evaluation of a situation to ensure a right spirit or intent in a matter.

It is important to understand that godly wisdom will take the lessons, failures, and practices of the past and consider them in light of present attitudes and actions to reveal future consequences. Wisdom that is properly heeded has the capability of changing a person's mind or perception about past and present actions, keeping them from future destruction.

The gift of the word of wisdom takes in the above scenario in regards to a person or even a body of believers. For example, Elijah brought a word of wisdom to King Ahab in regards to the murder of Naboth as a means to obtain his vineyard. Elijah uncovered the sins committed towards Naboth, and then he rebuked Ahab for his present attitude.

We see a point of instruction when Ahab was informed that his idolatry caused his present situation, which was described by Elijah as selling himself to work wickedness in God's sight. Because of the past sin and the present practice of evil, future judgment was pronounced upon Ahab.[2]

Ahab repented and changed his mind and his practices. Because he adhered to Elijah and humbled himself before God, God put off the judgment until the days of his son. In spite of his wickedness, Ahab responded wisely to Elijah's tough, but wise rebuke and warning. This reminds us that if wisdom is heeded, it has the capacity of producing wise decisions or acts that change future events.

In one incident, the Lord revealed that one of the young women in our Bible Study group was harboring destructive plans. As the Holy Spirit was bringing it to the light, He showed me the struggles of her past that had brought her to the present situation and the future consequences if she did not abort her present plans.

Upon confronting her, I shared with her that the Holy Spirit had revealed the destructive patterns of her past and her present delusion and where it was leading her. In the confrontation, the Lord continued to reveal the core of her struggles so we could properly instruct and minister to her in order to bring her to a correct perspective. Praise God for His faithfulness because she

---

[2] I Kings 21:17-29

aborted her plans; thereby, ceasing her present practices and avoiding devastating consequences.

In another situation, I had been working with a man who was trying to save his marriage. I had only heard his side and realized that his wife had her own version. After a few weeks of his prompting, she agreed to meet with both of us. Just before the meeting, the Holy Spirit gave me a word of wisdom concerning what was really going on in their marriage. Within seconds, He showed me the man's cruel mind games, the wife's battle to keep her sanity, and the inevitable end of their marriage if the man did not get a reality check about his cruelty and repent of his attitude and practices.

In our meeting, I explained what had been revealed to me. The wife was surprised at the insight, while her husband sat in a daze. I spent the next couple of hours trying to instruct the man in the ways of righteousness, while ministering to the battered wife. Sadly, the husband never recognized the mind games he was playing, but the wife felt a tremendous relief because she sensed God really understood her difficult plight. Needless to say, their marriage ended in divorce.

In another incident, a young man listened to his father cover up his past practices by justifying his present attitudes and activities with the Word of God. The Holy Spirit unveiled the intent or spirit behind his father, prompting the young man to challenge his father's perspective with the complete counsel of God's Word. Although his father maintained his right to practice wickedness, it silenced him for the rest of the night.

Another point of wisdom is that it always leads back to the character and mind of God. As wisdom is upheld, God's character is unveiled or glorified. In my experiences with the word of wisdom, I have come out with a greater sense of who God is.

God is aware of the history behind something and He knows the future, but He operates in the present. Godly wisdom brings the past and the present together to produce discretion as a means to change future results. Many times, we fail to realize that so much of the future is determined by the present. We see this in the case of King Josiah in 2 Chronicles 34.

King Josiah was considered a righteous king, but even in his righteousness he never realized how far away Israel had fallen from Jehovah God until Hilkiah, the priest, found the book of the Law. When the king heard the words of the Law, he tore his clothes in fear, humility, and repentance. He could see that the past actions of Israel demanded the wrath of God. He sent trusted men to Huldah, a prophetess, to inquire of the Lord.

The Lord assured the men, through the prophetess, that He would bring destruction upon Israel. But, because the king's heart was tender and he had humbled himself before Him, it would not happen in his lifetime.

Godly wisdom can change the future by changing the face of the present. God contends with the present in order to prolong or change the future. This is the main purpose behind the word of wisdom in the Body. It is to avoid experiencing the consequences for foolishness in the future.

This virtue of wisdom reminds me of how God introduced Himself to Moses, "I AM THAT I AM" (Exodus 3:14). God is the God of the present who works to bring the lessons of the past and the possibilities of the future together. This has the capacity of changing a person's present reality by enlarging their perception of Jehovah God. Every time I encounter and adhere to God's wisdom, I can almost hear His declaration, "I AM THAT I AM," and I know that if I line up to His unchanging reality or truth, He will change the focus of my life and my present reality.

Many Christians have unknowingly operated in the gift of wisdom. God uses the unsuspecting vessels to show His faithfulness to reach out to those with a searching, struggling heart. Ask the Lord if this is a gift that He would like to entrust to you. If He affirms it, give Him permission to use you in the area of His incredible wisdom. This gift will not only edify the Church, but it will also build you up as you grow in the knowledge of the Lord Jesus Christ.

11

WORD OF KNOWLEDGE

Many people confuse the word of wisdom, the word of knowledge, and prophecy with each other. It appears that they are similar; therefore, they are hard to distinguish from one another. However, these gifts are quite different from each other. Although the word of knowledge can appear to spill over into other gifts such as the word of wisdom and prophecy, it still stands distinct from the others.

According to *Strong's Concordance*, "knowledge" means to perceive, resolve, and understand. Perception points to the concept that the light comes in to reveal a matter, bringing understanding that will produce resolution and action.

The Apostle Paul told us that we can only see or perceive through a glass darkly.[1] Because of our flesh, we can only see shadows or outlines of something that, for the most part, is unseen to the physical eyes. This causes points of darkness and confusion that will leave a person struggling with unresolved issues. It can cause anger, sorrow, and despair.

The Holy Spirit uses the word of knowledge to bring understanding of a situation to a person who is struggling in their life. This gift can also reveal sin and corruption in the Church for spiritual correction. Therefore, it can be used to encourage,

---

[1] 1 Corinthians 13:12

reprove, rebuke, warn of pending judgment, intercede, and challenge a person in the area of salvation.

Unlike the word of wisdom that brings the past and future together in light of present-day decisions, the word of knowledge strictly operates in the present. The purpose for the word of knowledge is not to reveal the intent of something, but to identify with the person in their present plight, for the purpose of ministering, edifying, or contending for the faith.

Personal identification usually points to the edification of one person, but, in the area of the word of knowledge, it can be given to the entire body. It is God's way of saying to a believer or a body of believers, "You are (presently here)..." and bringing a situation to light in order to produce some type of ministry. Knowledge that is put into practice becomes wisdom.

We see the great prophet, Elisha, operating with this gift. In 2 Kings 5:20-27, Elisha's servant gave way to personal greed and pursued after Naaman to benefit from his offer to bestow Elisha with many gifts after his miraculous healing in the Jordan River. The prophet had turned his offer down, but his servant saw an opportunity to capitalize on God's miracle. Although he thought he was being wise and discreet, God showed Elisha what he had done.

When the servant stood before his master, Elisha asked him where he came from. I believe the prophet was giving his servant a chance to come clean, but, instead, he lied to his master. This probably sealed his doom as Elisha exposed his sinful actions and pronounced judgment upon him.

In 2 Kings 6:9-12, Elisha warned the king of Israel a couple of times about the destructive plans of the enemy. This supernatural protection that was in operation on behalf of Israel gained the attention of the king of the opposing side as he felt the betrayal came from within his own camp. Upon confronting his men, they assured him the information came from Elisha, the prophet, to the king of Israel who had also shown great wisdom by adhering to his warnings.

People have a tendency to wear masks to cover up various aspects of their personal lives. They silently struggle with issues that are swallowing them up in hopelessness. The Holy Spirit simply unmasks the person in order to bring correction, prevent consequences, or offer encouragement to stir up faith to receive His comfort and hope.

My friend, who has operated in the word of knowledge for years, sees pictures of where a person is spiritually. She has seen into the soul of a person in the areas of struggles, discouragement, and sin. On one occasion, the Lord revealed to her that a person was making plans that were destructive. She confronted her and the woman confessed to it, along with the battle that had been raging in her soul.

In another situation, the Lord showed my friend that a person was experiencing a deep loneliness that served as a deep ache in her soul. She shared the insight and encouraged the woman in the Lord.

Another lady had gone through terrible situations in her life. My friend, who was not even aware of this person's plight, came into the room and told her the Lord was going to cause her wounds to become badges of valor.

There was another individual who was having a problem with her aging father as he was becoming more difficult to handle. The Lord showed my friend that he had a tremendous amount of fear.

Another friend who operates in the gift of knowledge actually feels what the person is feeling, especially in the area of physical ailments. It is not unusual for her to feel some kind of pain or physical hindrance just before a meeting. She has to discern if the pain belongs to her or if it must be called out in the meeting. If she discerns that it must be called out, she knows God intends to heal the person. This personal identification in the word of knowledge is meant to actually stir up the faith of the recipient, as they must come forward in faith to receive the healing.

This brings us to another important aspect of the word of knowledge—what to do with it. A person must ask God what they are supposed to do with the knowledge He has entrusted to them. For my friend in the previous paragraphs, she knew that, once the ailment was properly discerned, she had the responsibility to call it out. However, in some cases, God may not want the information to be revealed as much as He wants the person to intercede in prayer.

In one situation, a saint was awakened in the middle of the night. She had a burden for a missionary friend. She was aware that the person was in some kind of grave danger. She interceded for her until the burden lifted. Later, she discovered that her friend was in a life-or-death situation due to political unrest in the country.

Unlike wisdom, certain knowledge should be kept hidden until the Holy Spirit gives permission to speak it. Some knowledge may be kept hidden from certain people while it is revealed to others around them in order to bring proper guidance. This is why people with this gift need to seek God's wisdom in how to properly exercise it and ensure the integrity of it.

In one situation, a woman was in a marital crisis. The Lord not only revealed what her husband was doing, but also lined out every step she was to take in order to counteract his destructive actions. As a result, to her husband's utter amazement, the woman kept one step ahead of his evil plans and actions.

As you can see, this type of knowledge is beyond human comprehension. It is supernatural and reveals how our all-knowing God uses it for the edification of the Church and for His glorification.

Have you benefited from this gift in the past? Perhaps He has or is entrusting it to you for the purpose of edification?

12

DISCERNING OF SPIRITS

Discerning of spirits is a gift that is shrouded in misunderstanding and confusion. For example, people who have this gift are usually accused of being judgmental or suspicious. People who are judgmental and suspicious often think that they are discerning. This confusion has caused those with the gift of discerning of spirits to close down their gift while allowing those with a critical spirit to freely reign under the guise of wisdom and discernment.

Therefore, it is important to understand the difference between judgmentalism and discernment. Discernment is the ability to detect a spiritual reality with senses other than vision. It is the ability to grasp or comprehend something that is obscure. According to my secular dictionary, man's judgment is nothing but an opinion that is held as an ultimate authority to a matter.[1]

The *Strong's Concordance* presents judgment as a determination, decision, or a decree for or against something. If the decision goes against something, it becomes the law that will accuse, condemn, or judge.[2]

As you compare discernment with man's judgment, you will see that they are on opposite poles. For example, discernment involves testing the spirits, while man's judgment is based on what

---

[1] Webster's New Collegiate Dictionary, © 1976 by G. & C. Merriam Co.
[2] #2919 and 2020

he hears and sees. Discernment evaluates the fruits of something, while judgment comes down to personal likes and dislikes. Discernment makes a righteous judgment in accordance with Jesus' words, "Judge not according to the appearance, but judge righteous judgment," while judgment comes down to how something makes a person feel.[3]

Discernment deals with the unseen world, while judgment evaluates according to earthly, fleshly things. Discernment discerns what is real, while judgment determines its own reality. Discernment is done for the sole purpose of the protection of souls, while judgment is to exalt and protect self. Discernment is spiritual in nature, while judgmentalism is personal in nature. Discernment sees into the unseen world, while judgmentalism has a critical eye that looks for and focuses on any discrepancy to justify personal ungodly attitudes, accusations, and criticism.

The Holy Spirit is behind discernment, while the natural man is behind judgmentalism. The intention of judging is to find and condemn what are considered unacceptable attitudes and actions. In most cases, it is the means to judge those considered inferior or too human for self-righteous people to accept. Discernment, on the other hand, is for the purpose of separating and distinguishing the spiritual from the natural.

Consider the table on the following page and determine if you are truly discerning or whether you have a critical spirit.

---

[3] John 7:24

DISCERNMENT	JUDGMENT
Test the Spirit.	Consider things according to what one hears and sees.
Evaluate the Fruits	Evaluates according to personal likes and dislikes.
Makes a righteous judgment.	Comes down to how something makes a person feel.
Deals with the unseen world.	Deals in the earthly, freshly realm.
Shows you what is real.	Determines what is reality according to its own personal preferences.
Protect souls and desires to properly minister to others	Protects self and has a critical eye.
Spiritual in nature.	Is carnal, fleshly, and personal in nature.
Holy Spirit is behind discernment and distinguishes spirit from natural.	The flesh is behind judgmentalism and will find fault and error.

It is important to point out that man's judgment consists of this combination:

Pride + vision and hearing = cemented opinions

Man often judges according to religious or self-righteous opinions that are considered doctrine. These opinions are nothing more than personal theology, but they determine attitude as to how a person will look at people and handle the pure doctrine of Jesus.

The combination for spirit is as follows:

Attitude +doctrine + fruits = spirit

95

Our attitude towards God and the doctrine we adhere to will influence the type of fruit our lives produce. The fruit reveals our disposition and will determine how we respond to that which opposes us. Judgmental pride sets up the attitude or prevailing mood, while spirit determines the environment or state of a matter. For example, if our attitude is that of arrogance, we will most likely hold to doctrine tightly and exalt it as the final authority. We will also have a critical, narrow-minded, and unteachable disposition.

Hebrews 5:13-14 gives us this insight about discernment, "…for everyone that useth milk is unskillful in the word of righteousness; for he is a babe. But strong meat belongeth to them that are of full age, even those who by reason of use have their senses exercised to discern both good and evil." Hebrews shows us that discernment is found among those who are matured in their relationship with God and in their skills with the Word of God.

Discerning good and evil is a process that entails a person testing the spirit as they consider the disposition and fruits in light of the Word of God. However, the gift of discerning of spirits is opposite. In other words, when a person has this gift, they immediately know something is wrong in an environment when they walk into a room or meeting. This revelation will set many signals off in the person who will immediately be put on guard. This will lead them to discern what is amiss in the environment.

Such discernment is not based on the person's personal perception, but an awareness of the spirit or environment behind leaders, churches, movements, and teachings.

Environment also represents foundation and practices. Wrong environments are dangerous, and not only will they harbor a wrong spirit, but they will establish a person on shifting sands of delusion and destruction.

Jesus uncovered the spirit behind Peter when he rebuked Him about going to the cross. "Get thee behind me, Satan. Thou art an offense unto me; for thou savorest not the things that are of God, but those that are of men" (Matthew 16:23).

We see the Apostle Peter revealing the motive behind the deceitful practices of Ananias and Sapphira in Acts 5:3-4,

> But Peter said, Ananias, why hath Satan filled thine heart to lie to the Holy Ghost and to keep back part of the price of the land? While it remained, was it not thine own? And after it was sold, was it not in thine own power? Why hast thou conceived this thing in thine heart? Thou hast not lied unto men, but unto God.

The gift of discerning spirits helps in deliverance by revealing the works of demonic spirits in a person. It helps discover and expose Satan's ministers as well as checks the plans of Satan. It exposes error and discerns miracles inspired by demons.

I have witnessed the value of this gift. I remember a woman with a bad spirit came into one of our meetings. My co-laborer warned me that she was there to gain attention and to find an inroad into the ministry. She actually saw herself as superior and was looking for a ministry to be exalted as a leader. As a result, I was able to avoid her traps and stopped her in her plans.

In another situation, we attended a church that had a wrong environment. The Holy Spirit immediately identified it as idolatry. As my friend observed the pastor, she recognized how the leader was trying to manipulate people out of their money for a fancy vacation.

We have walked out of meetings where both the spirit and teaching were wrong. In such cases, our spirits were grieved and we felt repulsed at the abuse of the Word. Likewise, sorrow filled us as we watched the sheep willingly embrace error on their way to the slaughter.

In one case, we ministered in a church in which both the spirit and environment were erroneous. After the meeting, my co-laborer, Jeannette, got deathly ill. It took some intense prayer for the wrong spirit and heaviness to lift from her, leaving her weak but able to recover from her ordeal.

Sadly, people with this gift are often abused by the people they are to protect. Many do not want their beliefs, leaders, and churches to be challenged. They would rather live in their delusion than face the fact that they have been duped because of the ignorance and pride in their own lives. The unreceptive attitudes of others cause those with the gift of discerning of spirits to either flee the situation or be driven to prayer until God gives them direction.

If you have this gift, take heart and make sure you are not closing it down. Give God permission to show you what is going on in the spiritual realm for your protection, as well as those you care about. Be available to not only warn others, but also to pray for their deliverance from the tentacles of Satan.

13

GIFT OF FAITH

The gift of faith belongs to the gifts of power. Jesus said that genuine faith has the ability to move mountains.[1] The real power in godly faith does not lie in the concept of faith, but in its ability to trust in the character of God, thereby, letting Him be God in matters. It is God who holds the power, while faith serves as a means or conduit by which God can show Himself mightily in and through a person, and as a result receive the proper glory in the end.

According to *Vine's Expository Dictionary of Biblical Words,* faith is a firm persuasion or conviction based on what a person hears. This is why faith comes by hearing and hearing by the Word of God, not by some method or practice.[2] It is active and will produce action, whether it is obedience, upright conduct, or a miraculous intervention from God. It is a firm confidence and child-like trust that will believe what God says because of who He is.

God gives all genuine faith; therefore, it comes from the outside of man and not from within. In other words, it cannot be conjured up by any personal attempts, faked, or spoken into being, no matter how sincere or fervent a person may be. It is not an idea, but an active walk that makes it an experience rather than an intellectual concept.

---

[1] Matthew 17:20
[2] Romans 10:17

Romans 12:3 states that God is the One who gives us a measure of faith. Granted, a person chooses to believe a matter is true. In other words, they choose to believe the Word of God is true. Such a choice is a matter of faith, but it finds its origins in the character of God or in His Word. Therefore, this measure of faith prepares and enables a person to take a step of obedience. Each step of obedience enlarges the person to be entrusted with greater measures of faith, allowing them to take larger steps of obedience before God. This is why the Christian life is considered a walk of faith, because what is not done by faith in the Christian life is considered sin.[3]

Hebrews 11:6 says that it is impossible to please God without this active faith. Real faith results in action because faith without action is dead and useless in the Christian life.[4] It is responsive to the Word of God. It simply chooses to believe everything God says as being absolute truth. It diligently seeks to know God and His will and way in order to respond properly in matters.

The faith walk is not a blind walk because it is based on the reality and character of a living, unchangeable God. It is a walk that is meek in its response, sober in its responsibilities, and confident in its actions. Ultimately, it allows God to fulfill His plan in and through a person's life.

The real measure of the faith a person possesses is determined by how much a person allows God to be God in challenging situations. The more confidence a person has in the character of God in the midst of testing, trials, and losses, the greater the potential for God to show Himself in a powerful way, bringing glory to Him. In fact, it is in the challenging times of life that faith is both tested and refined.[5]

---

[3] Romans 14:23; 2 Corinthians 5:7

[4] See James 2

[5] 1 Peter 1:6-7

Faith allows God to show His faithfulness to, in, and through a person. God's faithfulness greatly edifies the individual, while it has the potential to inspire and edify those who witness it in the lives of others. It is God's faithfulness that makes a person's testimony grow. This has been obvious in my own life.

After a four-year absence from people that I had worked and ministered with in the harvest field in the state of Washington, I was able to share with them the incredible faithfulness of God that I had experienced in those years. It was as if I had lived some of Hebrews 11 and could declare how God met me at every bend, turn, challenge, and crisis in my life. As I recounted God's numerous acts of intervention, the recipients were being strengthened in their own faith.

I shared with them the message of Psalm 89:1, "I will sing of the mercies of the LORD for ever: with my mouth will I make known thy faithfulness to all generations." I realize that this has been my consistent declaration about God for all the years I have known Him. Granted, I have failed to recognize it in the past and can easily take it for granted in the present, but I know His faithfulness has kept me in spite of my periods of faithlessness before Him.[6]

People have a tendency to get caught up in the idea of God's power, but powerful testimonies are based on the character and integrity that the Lord shows through His faithfulness. Every intervention, no matter how great or how small, is because of God's incredible faithfulness to deliver, reconcile, and restore His people.

Sadly, many people try to brainwash themselves about having faith, or they try to conjure it up in order to get God to move. Real faith is not a means by which to get God to move, but an avenue that encourages and allows God to move according to His will and purpose in and through His people.

---

[6] See 2 Timothy 2:11-13

Pseudo faiths are always based on man's design and not God's will. People often see faith as a magic wand or a means of controlling and manipulating God in a matter. Needless to say, these faiths undermine the faith that was first delivered to the saints.[7]

These pseudo faiths have perverted the gift of faith, opening a dangerous door to the occult. It has caused people to spiritualize faith by making it into a method or formula in wicked attempts to control God and obtain worldly blessings and success.

This demonically inspired faith is not only worldly, but also impulsive and morbid. People who are under the influence of this heretical faith make impulsive decisions that are based on emotional fervor to do something noble and spiritual for God.

God is put to a foolish test every time the flesh is involved in the concept or operation of faith, setting the person up as a fool. Once the person is deemed a fool, the individual will resort to becoming a silent, suffering martyr for God. This whole scenario is not only unfair to God, but it becomes morbid as this person believes they are suffering for the sake of Christ, when they are reaping the consequences of their religious foolishness.[8]

People need to test their responses. They need to discern if the flesh is driving them or if the Holy Spirit is leading them. This can easily be accomplished by testing everything with the Word of God.

There was an incident where a woman felt God was calling her into ministry. She immediately quit her job, bought clothes, and began to sit around waiting for the call. It never came and she fell into unbelief. If she had only studied the lives of Jesus and Paul, she would have recognized that there would be a time of preparation before the fulfillment of her call could materialize. Such preparation does not call for drastic change in lifestyle, but

---

[7] Jude 3
[8] Galatians 6:7-8; 1 Peter 4:15-17

learning to be faithful with what is already in front of you until the proper doors open.

In another situation, a man felt God was calling him to a higher life in God. He quit his job and started becoming very spiritual, but all he managed to do was put a burden on his family that brought them close to bankruptcy. In the process, the man lost respect and became a mockery and reproach to the Gospel.

People who are being driven will be impulsive in their decisions and pursuits. These sincere, but fleshly individuals will not only get ahead of God, but will become lost in their endeavors.

People who are being led by the Holy Spirit will be prepared to walk a matter out according to God's timing. They will learn discipline as they wait for the proper doors to open. They will be tested in their faithfulness to God as they deal with the drudgeries of everyday life. Ultimately, they will be ready to walk this life out under the leading of the Holy Ghost.

With this in mind, we can consider the gift of faith. It is not impulsive, but tempered by the understanding that God is about to do something extraordinary that is contrary to man's way of thinking and doing. For example, a friend had the assurance from God that He was going to move her family to our area where she would be actively involved with this ministry. This was not an emotional sentiment or an impulsive feeling based on desire, but an abiding truth that was already a reality to her. Needless to say, many did not share in her confidence. In fact, she was often criticized and mocked, but this conviction remained strong and steady.

She began to prepare for the move as projects were finished around the house that she and her husband had been remodeling. She even looked for housing in the area. I will never forget that the first house she looked at she immediately knew it was the house God had in mind for her and her family.

To make a long story short, almost two years after she had received the initial revelation from God, she and her family moved into the house the Lord had revealed was hers. There were various steps of faith that were taken by her and her family in those two years. The gift of faith that God gave her not only enabled her to endure skepticism and sustained her through uncertain times, but she continued to take what seemed like ridiculous steps, allowing God to fulfill His purpose in her life.

The gift of faith is actually opposite from the measure of faith. When God gives us the measure of faith, it is to enable us to take steps of obedience to enlarge us to receive what He has for us. On the other hand, the gift of faith immediately enlarges the individual so the person can be receptive to God's plan or promise, as they begin to respond accordingly in expectation of a future event.

It is important to point out that people must be prepared to even receive from God. One of the problems people have is recognizing what God has for them. This failure to recognize God's provision is due largely to the fact that people think in grandiose terms while God sovereignly operates in practical ways.[9] As people are looking for the miraculous to happen, God is quietly operating from a different angle. As a result, people miss what God is doing and become disillusioned in their spiritual lives.

The gift of faith enlarges a person enough so that they can immediately act upon it and eventually receive from God. It is in such cases as these that this gift has been known to result in healings and miracles.

For example, a person with the gift of healing may feel led to pray for a person's healing. As they step out in obedience to the Holy Ghost's leading, God immediately gives the intended recipient the gift of faith in order to receive the healing.

---

[9] Jeremiah 45:5

This is why God's sovereign will and man's faith are the two boundaries that all gifts of power work within. It must be God's will to ensure something takes place and man's willingness to respond according to obedience or in preparation to receive God's blessings or promises by faith.

The gift of faith makes a person wide open for God to do the impossible. The Holy Spirit has given both Jeannette and me this gift at different times to accomplish some amazing feats through us. In one incident, we had the opportunity to go to Georgia for a free promotional package for our book and her art. Immediately, we both knew that God wanted us to go, but we didn't have the money for the airline tickets.

The unwavering knowing in our spirits about the matter was nothing more than the gift of faith. In response to the gift of faith, we began to inquire about the cost of airline tickets. Although the money was not there, we were not deterred from knocking on doors until the right one miraculously opened.

One day, Jeannette was led to call a most unlikely individual and ask him and his wife to pray about the Georgia trip. The next morning, when we entered our office, we were greeted with a phone call from this man. He informed us that the airlines had informed him that very morning that he had accumulated enough mileage plus in all of his traveling, that he was donating half of them to us so we could fly to Georgia.

Faith allows God to show Himself in powerful and unsuspected ways. It is not amazing that God does the miraculous, but He always does things in a surprising manner. Therefore, you never know how and when He will do something. However, you can be sure of one thing. If God truly said it, it is already a reality.

This is why, in our faith walk, we occasionally remind Him, "God, you said..." We know without a doubt He will do what He has declared.

It is important to keep faith in perspective. There are many pseudo faiths being presented that will prevent the growth of real faith or sabotage the gift of faith within the Body.

If you have been given the gift of faith, respond according to God's leading. Avoid getting ahead of Him and begin to knock on all doors, trusting that He will open the right one at the right time. Even though you will be assured of seeing God move in some incredible ways, know that the most sustaining reality is that HE IS FAITHFUL!

14

HEALING AND MIRACLES

When people think of healing and miracles, they are reminded of power that is operating in the supernatural that will produce the miraculous. Sadly, many people chase after this power by pursuing after the gifts of healing and miracles.

There are some major reasons why people pursue the supernatural, and one of the reasons is sensationalism. Power of the supernatural not only serves as a means to attract people to the unexplainable, but it also entertains them as well.

Jesus encountered this same attitude in His lifetime. Sensationalism was prevalent in the Roman Empire. They went to great lengths to entertain the people. Not only did they lull them spiritually asleep and cause their fleshly appetites to become insatiable, but they also caused them to operate in an unrealistic world.

When Jesus encountered Herod on the last trek of His journey to Calvary, Herod was interested in what He could do, and not in His identity, guilt, or innocence. Luke 23:8 reveals this attitude, "And when Herod saw Jesus he was exceedingly glad; for he was desirous to see him for a long time, because he had heard many things of him; and he hoped to have seen some miracle done by him." When Jesus did not perform a miracle for Herod, he and his men treated Him with contempt, by arraying Him with a beautiful robe in order to mock Him.[1]

Self-serving pursuits into the supernatural often set people up as they put God to a foolish test and bring a reproach on Him. When people are in the flesh, they can be foolish and make impulsive, fleshly declarations about Him that are not according to His will. Such people who operate in this manner will often become a Herod in attitude as their pursuit turns into contempt and mockery towards the One who refuses to perform according to their whims.

It is easy to put God to a foolish test, thinking that surely, He will not allow believers to look foolish and bring doubt upon His character. The truth is that God will not keep people from looking foolish to protect His reputation. He will allow the foolish to pay the price of their arrogance to teach them valuable lessons.

The overemphasis of the supernatural is due, in part, because God's people make the mistake of putting *faith in what He can do instead of who He is.* In fact, people transpose their own ideas of what they would do if they were all-powerful onto God. They forget God's power is just one aspect of His character. He is so much more, and all of His attributes contribute to His intervention in people's lives. Therefore, His intervention is not based on His ability to do great things, but on His great character to work the impossible in a situation that will cause spiritual growth for His followers and bring Him glory.

Due to the American mindset, the combination of power, attraction, and entertainment plays quite nicely into these types of religious pursuits. The difference is that God is tacked on, giving such pursuits a noble, religious quality, while covering up a fleshly, demonic hype that often proves to serve as a wicked covering in which these people hide their sin of unbelief.

---

[1] Luke 23:11

Another reason that the gifts of healing and miracles are sought after is because they supposedly confirm the person's spiritual authority and claims. Mark 16:17-18 states,

> And these signs shall follow them that believe; In my name shall they cast out devils; they shall speak with new tongues; They shall take up serpents; and if they drink any deadly thing, it shall not hurt them; they shall lay hands on the sick, and they shall recover.

The Scriptures in Mark are in relation to the preaching of the Gospel. They state that certain signs will follow those who believe. In other words, these signs will be a natural result of those who believe the Gospel, and in turn, preach it to others. These signs are meant to confirm the message, not the vessel.[2]

This brings us back to the real test of signs and wonders. Is the person preaching the true Gospel, and what spirit is in operation? The Holy Spirit will make His presence felt when Jesus is lifted up in His glory and work, while another spirit will direct people away from the only way to heaven, causing them to put their reliance elsewhere.

There is no place in Scripture where signs and wonders serve as proof of someone's validity other than Christ. In fact, people who stress the supernatural over Jesus Christ and the Christian's commission to preach the Gospel and make followers of Christ reveal they are of another spirit.

Jesus made this statement about those who seek after signs and wonders in Matthew 16:4, "A wicked and adulterous generation seeketh after a sign; and there shall no sign be given unto it, but the sign of the prophet, Jonah." Jesus clearly revealed that only those who are wicked and adulterous (spiritual harlotry) seek after signs, rather than the reality of God.

It is important to test the spirit behind signs and wonders. In the end days, there will be many signs and wonders, but they will

---

[2] See Mark 16:20

be counterfeits along with the ones who perform them.[3] Matthew 24:24 gives us this warning, "For there shall arise false Christs, and false prophets, and shall show great signs and wonders, insomuch that, if it were possible, they shall deceive the very elect." Christians should never seek after signs and wonders. Rather, they need to seek God and know that He is the source of all truth and spiritual life.

Let us now consider the gift of healing.

Gift of Healing

The gift of healing is totally an intervention on God's part that is marked by His sovereignty. On the other hand, man's part in the gift of healing involves the measure of faith and not the gift of faith. The gift of healing will be an act of obedience on the part of the person to pray for healing.

This is why the gift of healing is a separate gift from the gift of faith. Many people believe that the person who is praying for the healing of someone is operating in a gift of faith when, in reality, it is nothing more than a step of obedience. At times God has been known to give the gift of faith to the recipient to receive the healing, but the gifts of faith and healing work independently from each other.

This is why people who feel they have the gift of healing must discern if they are being pushed, driven by impulsive feelings, or are clearly being led by the Holy Spirit to pray for a person's healing. It is easy to discern if a person is being pushed or driven by overwhelming emotions, zeal, or sentiment because they will have a sense of infallibility. This person will actually perceive that this sentiment is the gift of faith and will see it as a means to accomplish anything as long as that feeling remains.

---

[3] 2 Thessalonians 2:9-10

Now, notice where the focus is. It is not on God's purpose or greatness, but on the person who possesses the infallible feeling. This person does not realize that God is clearly missing, and that they are operating according to emotional zeal or fervor that is setting them up for disaster. This fervor is fleshly and operates on an earthly plane of sentiment and it will ultimately put God to a foolish test.

The Apostle Paul warned us of such zeal in Romans 10:2, "For I bear them record that they have a zeal for God, but not according to knowledge." Obviously, people who operate on this level do not understand the character, way, and will of God.

Christians who understand and properly operate in any of the gifts of power will know that it has nothing to do with them. They are just the vessels through which God's power will flow. They do not have a sense of infallibility when operating in the gift, but an awareness of how great, powerful, and faithful God is. In fact, they will often feel small, insignificant, and powerless, causing them to fling themselves on God to allow Him do His bidding through them.

Believers who properly operate in the gift of healing have admitted feeling reluctant, sober, or afraid to pray for a person's healing because they felt no power within themselves to do anything. The reason for this is because the Holy Spirit is leading them, and they are simply being obedient to be used as a conduit or instrument of the Holy Ghost.

In one incident, my friend was asked to pray for an individual whom she was not fond of. This person had liver cancer and definitely needed God to step on the scene. My friend reluctantly obeyed and prayed for her. The lady was healed and God received the glory.

I often instruct people who feel led to pray for someone's healing to use discretion when approaching the individual. It is unwise to tell the person anything other than that God has impressed them to pray for them. The reason for this discretion is that one is never sure what God wants to accomplish until the Holy Spirit reveals it. The healing might not be obvious, or it may be something other than what can be perceived with the eyes. The healing may be spiritual rather than physical, and it may encompass various things.

There are three types of healings found in the Word. The greatest of these healings is spiritual healing.

Jesus came to bring spiritual healing. Although He healed many physical ailments, His greatest desire was to make people spiritually whole. It is important to point out that He healed many physical ailments, but it was only the people's response of faith in Him that made them whole.

For example, the woman with the issue of blood displayed the gift of faith as she pressed through to touch the hem of Jesus' garment. Jesus had the power to heal her physically, but, because of her faith, He made this statement to her, "Daughter be of good comfort; thy faith hath made thee whole" (Matthew 9:20-22). As you can see, her physical healing was not the same as her being made spiritually whole.

This woman's healing went beyond the physical into the spiritual realm. Physical healing may change the physical quality of a person's life, but it does not make them spiritually whole. People can be healed physically, but be spiritually lost. The key to spiritual healing is that faith not only reaches out to Jesus, but it touches Him in such a way that it connects to the very heart and goal of God—reconciliation and restoration.

Luke 4:18 talks about spiritual healing,

> The Spirit of the Lord is upon me, because he hath anointed me to preach the gospel to the poor, he hath sent me to heal the broken-hearted, to preach deliverance to the captives, and recovering of sight to the blind, to set at liberty them that are bruised.

112

Jesus presented five different spiritual conditions in this verse that not only needed to be addressed, but healed. These spiritual conditions are the result of the fallen disposition of man and sin that can only be dealt with on a spiritual level. Poverty of any type causes oppression and mental anguish, while a broken heart is hard to bear. Oppression can break a person's spirit, while spiritual blindness can cause hopelessness. Spiritual bruising or contusions can cause unexpected pain caused by memories, soreness of the emotions, and other problems.

Jesus was anointed to address these conditions and managed to deal with the source of them on the cross. This was brought out in Isaiah 53:4-5. Isaiah 53:4 reveals how Jesus bore the fruits of spiritual poverty, broken hearts, captivity, blindness, and bruising by taking on our griefs and carrying our sorrows. Isaiah 53:5 refers to the source of these griefs and sorrows—transgression and iniquities. These spiritual ailments caused enmity with God that caused separation. Jesus not only addressed these ailments, but He brought healing and peace on the cross. Isaiah 53:5 summarizes it in this manner, "...and with his stripes we are healed."

One of the problems surrounding healing is that most Christians think in terms of physical healing and not spiritual. Isaiah 6:10 shows the need for spiritual healing, "Make the heart of this people fat, and make their ears heavy, and shut their eyes; lest they see with their eyes, and hear with their ears, and understand with their heart, and convert, and be healed." Many people believe that God does not want them physically sick when, in reality, God's heart is to see them spiritually healed or saved. Physical sickness lasts only for a season compared to a spiritual healing that will last an eternity.

This brings us to physical healings. There is an erroneous belief that physical ailments are a result of sin and a lack of faith.

Granted, sin such as unforgiveness can cause physical problems, but not all ailments are a result of sin or unbelief.

Jesus made this quite clear in John 9:2-6 when his disciples asked Him who sinned to make the man blind, the man or his parents. Jesus answered, "Neither hath this man sinned, nor his parents: but that the works of God should be made manifest in him."

This Scripture verse clearly shows that not all physical ailments are associated with man's fallen condition; rather, it could be marked with God's eternal purpose. God actually uses physical challenges to manifest His work in and through people. This could mean a lot of different things. For instance, God can use physical challenges to do a deep work in a person's soul like He did with Job. Job came out knowing God in greater ways.[4]

I have seen this in various cases such as that of Joni Erickson Tada. God could have healed her, but, instead, He showed her that He manifests His glory through her physical weakness in a greater measure, enabling her to minister to others in incredible ways.

It is important to point out that Jesus did not heal everyone. At the pool of Bethesda, many sick people were waiting for the miraculous to happen. Jesus only healed one man out of many.[5] This, once again, reminds us that God does not heal people for the sake of healing, but that He operates according to an eternal plan and purpose.

Sometimes physical ailments are caused by spiritual oppression, as in the case of the daughter of Abraham in Luke 13:10-16. This is why a person who operates in this gift must not assume anything until the Holy Spirit reveals the type of healing and the source behind the affliction. It might require spiritual deliverance.

---

[4] Job 42:1-6
[5] John 5:1-16

The third type of healing is physical death. If a person is a saint, physical death is the ultimate healing. 2 Corinthians 5:8 states, "We are confident, I say, and willing rather to be absent from the body, and to be present with the Lord."

Psalm 116:15 gives us God's perspective on the death of a saint, "Precious in the sight of the LORD is the death of his saints!" People enter the door of physical death through accidents, catastrophes, and physical illness. It is God's way of ushering the saint into His everlasting presence.

Christians need to remember that we are simply passing through this world and our destination is of an eternal nature.[6] This world is simply a place of testing, training, and preparation for that which will be everlasting.

Each person is preparing for heaven or hell according to the path they are traveling.[7] This is why saints must hold lightly to the things of earth and trust God with all obstacles, including physical ailments. They need to realize that each challenge prepares each of them for that blessed time when they will enter through the door of physical death and embrace the Lord in everlasting joy and adoration.

Has the Holy Spirit used you in this gift? Be wise and discerning as to His leading. Never allow yourself to be pushed or driven by emotional fervor, putting God to a foolish test and bringing a reproach on your character and testimony.

Gift of Miracles

Some Christians express surprise that gifts of healing and miracles are separate. It is true that healing is a miracle, but miracles encompass the rest of God's supernatural intervention on behalf of man.

---

[6] 1 Peter 2:11
[7] Matthew 7:13-14

One of the challenges that occurs in the area of miracles is that many Christians have an improper perception about them. Therefore, it is important to establish what constitutes a miracle. We know it is supernatural in nature. In other words, it works outside of what is natural. It supersedes physical laws, the elements of nature, and man's abilities.

The perception that many have of miracles comes down to such acts as the parting of the Red Sea, the calming of the storms, causing the sun to stand still, and the feeding of the 5,000. These miracles definitely stand out, but what many fail to realize is that these miracles were in *proportion to the need or situation.*[8]

For example, it was more practical to part the Red Sea for thousands to cross over than to enable each of them to walk on water as Jesus did with Peter. Since there were 5,000 people to feed, God simply fed them by multiplying some fish and bread, rather than pouring manna out of heaven as He did for the children of Israel. Therefore, providing the needs of one person who has no other means is just as much of a miracle as the feeding of the 5,000 because it is beyond personal abilities to solve the problem.

God works in practical and personal ways. When God performs a miracle, He might be meeting a need, moving an obstacle, straightening out crooked paths, or pushing back storms and enemies. He meets people right where they are.

I encountered God's miraculous intervention in the way of healing. The Lord was calling us to minister in the Seattle, Washington area. I had injured my knee when I was in the Navy. It served as my barometer, warning me of impending weather change.

I had briefly mentioned to God how the weather in Washington would have a tremendous affect on my injured knee. A couple of weeks later, I was in a prayer meeting with some friends. One

---

[8] Exodus 14:13-22; Joshua 10:12-14; John 6:1-21

friend just reached over and began to pray for me. Suddenly, the power of God came down through my head and shot down to my knee. Within seconds, it lifted, but my knee was completely healed.

It struck me that God touches our lives when we are either at a point of desperate need or not expecting it at all. I had not specifically asked Him to heal my knee, and my friend was not praying for my knee. However, God sovereignly stepped on the scene during a time of intercession and showed His grace and power in an unexpected way.

In my walk with God, I have experienced and been part of many miracles. I have watched God step on the scene and heal and restore lives and relationships as well as save people from inevitable destruction. I learned that any willing vessel that has child-like faith and is humble, broken, or prayerful can serve as a conduit through which His miracles can occur.

An evangelist shared a personal experience where he had witnessed a man collapsing and dying of a heart attack in one of the major airports in America. At the time, the evangelist was with other godly men waiting for a flight. One of them suggested they all pray for God to intervene and resurrect the man. The evangelist admitted that he reluctantly placed his small finger on the man in front of him as some of the others fervently prayed. Within seconds breath came back into the man, and he was restored back to life.

We often forget how the fervent prayers of Elijah ended a three-year drought and that Jesus asked the Father to honor His requests such as the feeding of the 5,000 and the resurrection of the dead.[9] We forget the miraculous because we fail to see the practical side of God's intervention. This failure is due to our expectations of the miraculous that are often sensational and self-

---

[9] Mark 6:41; James 5:17-18

serving in nature. As a result, many unbelieving or skeptical people chalk God's miracles up to coincidence.

It is important to stress that God does not exploit His power to entertain people, nor does He toy with people in order to impress or control them. He does not do the miraculous to prove Himself. Rather, He does the miraculous because of Who He is. Anytime God intervenes on behalf of man, it becomes a touch of the supernatural, which makes it a miracle. It is for this reason I often remind people that the incredible and miraculous is normal to God, but is not normal to us.

People's motives to witness or be part of miracles are often fleshly and worldly. They want God to prove Himself, defend His reputation, or back up their claims with some supernatural act. God will do none of these. God does the miraculous because it ultimately fulfills His purpose or brings glory to Him.

Jesus made this clear in the raising of Lazarus in John 11. He was informed that Lazarus was sick and He needed to come to heal him. Jesus purposely tarried a couple of days after declaring, "This sickness is not unto death, but for the glory of God that the Son of God might be glorified in it" (John 11:4).

God never steps outside of His character, will, purpose, or promises. Granted, He does the unexpected to surprise you at times. The unexpected gives you a sense that it is not only a matter of showing you how aware He is of you, but that it brings such pleasure to His heart when your response is that of child-like excitement and adoration.

There are three facts you need to remember at all times about God's intervention on behalf of man.

   1) God has nothing to prove because He is God. He is not on some pride trip as man would be in His position, but rather He is silently and patiently working behind the scenes to bring about a desired end.

2) His goal is not to straighten up men, but rather to save them.[10]   When we think of power, we think in terms of getting people to see it our way. I have been guilty of this emphasis. In the past, I have used my prayers to try to stir God up to line people up by causing them to see it my way. Eventually, He showed me how self-serving my emphasis was. After all, it is not a matter of getting people to agree with me, but believing in their hearts the truth about His provision of Jesus. Sadly, our pride causes us to not only miss the heart of God, but to fail to become part of His work and harvest.

3) God could create a solution out of the dust or air, but He wants to take what is available and multiply it. The key to multiplication in the kingdom of God is being faithful with what God has given you and offering it to Him in faith like the boy who offered his lunch in John 6. This small lunch was multiplied to feed 5,000.[11] We often consider God's intervention in light of the unseen or abundance instead of realizing that God can take something we often consider small or insignificant and multiply it, bringing Him glory.

This brings us to the greatest miracle—the salvation of man's soul. We often look for miracles outside of what God accomplishes in the humble heart of the repentant man. The concept of the salvation of man points to something beyond personal abilities. Jesus clearly brought this out when His disciples asked Him who could be saved. He said, "With men this is impossible, but with God all things are possible" (Matthew 19:26).

If you have truly received God's provision of salvation through Jesus Christ, you need to realize that you are a walking miracle. Every believer is a living testimony not only of God's commitment, but also His ability to do the impossible on behalf of man.

---

[10] Luke 9:56
[11] John 6:9

If you are a Christian, you also need to realize that you have been a part of the miraculous. God is still in the business of miracles. Take this time and consider the ways in which God has touched your life in practical, but miraculous ways. Begin to bring honor and glory to the One who is worthy of all praise and worship.

15

GIFT OF PROPHECY

The inspirational gifts are found at the core of the conflict over the gifts of the Spirit. It is as though the debate over these gifts, especially the gift of tongues, has brought into question the validity of the other gifts of the Spirit. Amazingly, it is what Scripture said in regard to the gift of tongues that made me consider and study the gifts of the Spirit in an unbiased way.

1 Corinthians 14:39 instructs, "Wherefore, brethren, covet to prophesy, and forbid not to speak with tongues." This Scripture showed me that believers must covet the best of the gifts. For example, in the category of the gifts of revelation, wisdom would be the most desired, while, in the gifts of power, faith ranks in importance, but prophecy should be coveted in the gifts of inspiration. Once again, I could see no indication that the Church was to overlook or ignore them.

After I realized that I was being instructed to covet certain gifts, I was also being told **not to forbid tongues**. I had a choice. I could ignore this Scripture, and hold on to denominational beliefs and teachings about these gifts, which would bring me into disobedience to the Word of God, or, I could accept what it said and seek out God's perspective on them. Needless to say, I chose the latter.

As I pondered the controversy centered on the inspirational gifts, I started to see the real core surrounding the validity of the gifts. It actually comes down to control.

Christians have unknowingly operated in the gifts of revelation and power, and it is easy to accredit these occurrences to intellectual wisdom, insight, blessings, or coincidence. However, a person cannot consider the inspirational gifts in light of the normal, especially the gift of tongues. If the inspirational gifts are valid for today, they speak of something outside of the control of man, making them supernatural in nature.

Man fears what he cannot control or understand. This is clearly seen in how people respond to the gift of tongues. For example, they can ascribe prophecy to imagination and interpretation of tongues as part of the show, but what do you do with those frightening tongues that can throw people into confusion and cause one to sweat as they hear something they cannot control or understand. In the scheme of things, one has to either do away with all the gifts, even though it is clear we have need of such insights that come from wisdom, knowledge, and faith, deem such practices as fanaticism and, therefore, from Satan, or consider the possibilities that the Bible is true and these gifts are still available and in operation. The problem with the gift of tongues is that it proves there are things outside of man's understanding and control that must be accepted on the basis of faith and obedience.

This inability to control makes one feel vulnerable to the supernatural. The abuses in the area of the inspirational gifts have not helped people's fears, doubts, and debates about the gifts of the Spirit.

The inspirational gifts are the most abused of the nine gifts. It is not unusual to see people step over the line into the fleshly and demonic in these gifts. Once individuals begin operating with fleshly hype or under the influence of a demonic spirit, chaos takes over that can border between fanaticism and insanity. Such chaotic actions will bring a reproach to Christianity, as well as drive others away in fear and skepticism.

I believe this is why there are some stringent guidelines surrounding the inspirational gifts. These guidelines not only guard against the counterfeits, but they establish boundaries to ensure the integrity of these gifts. For example, there should not be more than three messages of prophecy and tongues in each meeting. Each prophecy must be confirmed by the Word of God and by fulfillment of it down to the most menial details. The tongues must be interpreted for the edification of those present.[1]

After being in meetings where these gifts were abused, I could see the necessity of such boundaries. People treat spiritual matters as if there are no boundaries or rules and as if anything goes, as long as it appears to be spiritual or supernatural.

In one meeting, fleshly hype began to replace the moving of the Holy Spirit. I watched the pastor as concern and sternness came over his countenance. The next Sunday, the pastor took the opportunity to instruct people and warn them that chaotic behavior would not be tolerated. It is important that, if gifts are in operation, the leadership must be alert, discerning, and quick to instruct as to the gifts' proper use to ensure order.

This brings us back to the subject of control. If these gifts are of God, how do you control them? You cannot unless you happen to be the vessel that refuses to vocalize the inspiration that is being given to you. It is not up to man to control God. It is simply his responsibility to test all messages, and, if they are of God, he needs to receive them, regardless of the method or the vessel God may use.

It is not unusual to see people try to dictate to God according to their understanding and comfort zones. These people test things according to how something makes them feel. If they feel uncomfortable, they automatically deem it as erroneous and close

---

[1] Deuteronomy 18:20-22; 1 Corinthians 14:27-33

down. They never get to the stage where they actually test the message according to the spirit and Word.

As a result, many miss valuable insight, encouragement, and warnings. They not only close themselves down to the possibilities of God speaking directly to them in this unusual manner, but they forbid the practice of these gifts, such as tongues, coming into opposition of Scripture.

This brings us to the other aspect of the inspirational gifts—understanding God's use of them. People cannot understand why God uses a method that appears foolish and insignificant to them to get His point across. 1 Corinthians 1:27-29 explains why God uses such methods,

> But God hath chosen the foolish things of the world to confound the wise; and God hath chosen the weak things of the world to confound the things which are mighty; And base things of the world, and things which are despised, hath God chosen, yea, and things which are not, to bring to nought things that are, That no flesh should glory in his presence.

We are not meant to understand the reason of God, but we do have a responsibility to embrace what is of God by faith. The gifts of the Spirit are meant to bring God's perspective to a matter and the gift of prophecy is no exception.

Prophecy is the one consistent work of the Holy Spirit that can be found in the five positions, the gifts of grace, and the gifts of the Spirit. In the case of prophecy in the relationship to the five positions established for the Church, the prophet is meant to guard the spiritual well-being of the Body. This may mean forthtelling to bring instruction or foretelling in order to warn. In the gifts of grace, prophecy often points to an inspired preacher who only speaks according to the spiritual condition of the hearers.

The gift of prophecy can operate within both the boundaries of forth-telling or foretelling. It implies one is definitely speaking on behalf of someone else. In this atmosphere, a person is speaking on behalf of God.

In forth-telling, it is often used as a means to encourage or exhort the body or a person. In foretelling, it serves as a means of warning with the intention to tear down with truth with the intent to build up in godliness. This gift deals with the present in order to confirm or change the direction of a person or local body by pointing to future promises or consequences.

As you study the importance of the gift of prophecy, you will realize that one of the responsibilities of the Holy Spirit is to show us things to come.[2] Obviously, if we close down the avenue of gifts, we will prevent the Holy Spirit from preparing us for the future. Without preparation, we will not be able to stand, withstand, and endure to the end.

As pointed out, there are different emphases of these gifts. The word of wisdom emphasizes God as the great I Am; therefore, one must line up to His instructions, while the word of knowledge deals with the present by stating, "You are (here)." The gift of faith will declare, "God, you said," while the gift of prophecy has God declaring: "I will (carry this out)."

Prophecy is often confused with the gifts of the word of wisdom and the word of knowledge, but each gift is designed to address and change different aspects of the person (or body of believers). For example, the word of wisdom is directed at the person's perception and is meant to change how a person perceives reality, especially in the area of God. The word of knowledge meets a person in their present situation with the intention of changing present reality. The gift of prophecy is meant to minister to the whole body or man with the intent of establishing or changing the person or body's direction or inward environment.

We see this in the case of Israel. Many times God exposed the Israelites' rebellious and idolatrous condition in order to warn them

---

[2] John 16:13

of future judgment. God's goal was to bring them to repentance in hopes of postponing or warding any judgment off. As we know, they did not heed Him; therefore, they had to drink the bitter dregs of their folly.

One must point out the encouragement that was intermingled with the pronouncement of judgment upon Israel. Although the judgments would be carried out, God promised them that, one day, He would restore national Israel and that their king would rule over them. I have read accounts of how the Jewish people have clung to these promises in trying times because they know if God said it, He will do it.

I have witnessed this in my own life and heard various testimonies of God's integrity to His Word. I remember an incident where God promised a woman that He would save her husband. Her husband later died and she felt betrayed because she had not witnessed any conversion. It was not until five years later that she learned from a stranger who was trying to touch base with her husband that God had fulfilled this promise. As they compared notes, the woman learned that this man had caught a ride with her husband. The Lord had prompted him to share the Gospel. As a result, he had led this woman's husband to Christ the very night he was killed in a car accident.

Prophecies can have conditions that one must meet before they can be fulfilled. My co-laborer, Jeannette, prophesied over a man concerning his potential in the kingdom of God, but it carried a condition. Before God could make him this godly man, he had to get into the Word of God. The man failed to do his part and today remains in the same pigpen of hopelessness.

It is also important that people do not become impulsive or presumptuous about a prophecy. In one situation, a man was given a personal prophecy that he decided to bring about in his own strength. He packed up his family and went in search of the fulfillment of it, only to become disillusioned and financially close to ruin. Prophecies are brought forth when the right environment or timing are in place, such as in the case of Jesus' birth.

Regardless of how spiritual a prophecy may sound, it must be properly tested. Prophecies often confirm what a person already knows to be true in their spirit. For example, if a person brings a prophecy to you, it will be in accordance to what God has already shown you.

In one incident, a man brought a prophecy of judgment upon me. Immediately, I knew it was not of God, because it failed three important criteria that are clearly brought out by the Old Testament prophets.

1) It was out of order. God has an order when He pronounces any type of judgment. He will first always expose sin and call for repentance before He pronounces judgment. This person did not expose any sin, nor did he call for repentance. God's heart is to always bring reconciliation, not judgment.[3] Repentance will change a person's direction, thwart judgment, and bring reconciliation. Therefore, a prophecy that lacks both order and God's heart is not from Him.

2) There was no confirmation in my spirit. God uses such gifts as prophecy to confirm something that He has already laid on a person's heart. At the time of this man's so-called "prophesy", God was not convicting me of sin, nor was He calling me to repentance.

3) The person's spirit was wrong. I sensed the prophecy this man was giving me was more about his own jealousies and personal arrogance than it was about me. He did not seem concerned for me spiritually, and almost appeared to glory in the perspective that I was coming down. This is not a spirit of meekness and compassion. It is God's will to bring everyone to repentance in order to avoid judgment.

---

[3] Luke 9:56; 2 Corinthians 5:18-19

Therefore, He does not glory in bringing people down, nor should His followers. In fact, they should tremble at such prospects, for they could fall in the same traps and experience the same judgments.[4]

If a prophecy is of God, it is not up to individuals to fulfill it. People must wait on God to bring it about. Believers' responsibility in such times is to be faithful stewards with what they have been entrusted with until God brings forth the prophecy. Also, prophecies that have conditions will not be fulfilled until the person meets them. This is why learning to be faithful on a daily basis in your life before God ensures that all godly prophecies will be brought about for God's glory.

Prophecies can also be improperly exalted in ways that will not only result in abuse, but will be idolatrous in nature. I know of a woman who kept all of her prophecies in a notebook and would refer to them as if they were the Bible. It was as if her whole life hinged on and operated according to these prophecies. Christians must never operate according to prophecies or promises, but according to the leading of the Spirit and the righteous instructions and boundaries of the Word of God.

Over the years, I have received various prophecies. I have put them on the shelf and continued with the work that was before me. Prophecies can be abstract; therefore, they can be fulfilled without a person even knowing it until they look back. It was only years later that I realized that most of these prophecies were fulfilled without me even realizing it.

In one prophecy, I was told that I would have a time of pinnacle where I would move into my gift without sweat. It was not until three years later, when I once again heard that part of the prophecy on tape, that I realized it had been fulfilled in an unusual way. I had been moving into a certain gift without any effort or

---

[4] 1 Corinthians 10:12; 2 Timothy 2:24-26

sweat for over a year. The most amazing part of this time was that it took place at our office that was located in a building called the "Pinnacle Building." This showed me that the fulfillment of valid prophecies simply confirmed that I was on the right path and to continue to walk in that direction.

This brings us to the issue of personal prophecies. Do they exist? Yes, they do, but there are a lot of abuses and misunderstandings in this area. There are numerous people running around claiming to be prophets with a personal prophecy for anyone they encounter. Many of these people are nothing more than fortune-tellers who use Christ as their authority, a familiar spirit as their source, vain imaginations as their glass ball, and empty promises as a means to feed the flesh and pride of those who believe them.

Today, there are a lot of false prophecies floating around. Sadly, many people have believed them, causing devastation and unbelief in their life.

One man received various prophecies that he would marry a well-known woman. This man clung to this prophecy because it fed his fantasy. But realistically, this woman would have never given this man the time of day. Life basically passed this man by as he held on to the fantasy, rather than face reality and live his life for God, entrusting Him with the events of his life.

All prophecies must be tested. Each prophecy must have the evidence of the Spirit of God by upholding the Word of God. If a prophecy is contrary to God's character or His Word, it must be rejected.

This is why prophecies must be put on the shelf until God brings them forth. People who try to fulfill their own prophecies or cling to false prophecies will be made to look the part of a fool, rather than obedient servants of God. If a prophecy is false, a person does not want to cling to it regardless of how it might serve their purpose because it is not of God. Rather, the prophecy is a lie that will result in disillusionment.

God does keep His word. He is able to move heaven and earth, but it is on His terms, not ours. We also must make sure a prophecy is from God and refuse to believe or toy with anything that would give us false hope or lead us down a path of delusion.

When godly prophecy is maintained in purity and integrity, it will serve as a vital part of the Church's edification. This is why 1 Thessalonians 5:20 instructs, "Despise not prophesyings." According to *Strong's Exhaustive Concordance*, the word "prophesying," in this Scripture, points to prediction. In this text, we see the Church must not despise foretelling. Predictions from God can be quite unnerving for those who are not used to them, but they must be embraced to ensure faithfulness and preparation for what is coming down the tracks.

Two days before Jesus was offered up on the cross, He predicted the events that would lead up to the end of the age. His reason for this was not to scare people, but to encourage them to be spiritually ready to stand, endure, and patiently wait in confidence for His return.[5]

As Jesus shared hard truths about the days of great tribulation, encouragement was interwoven within the darkness. The hope surrounding these events is that it will bring the Light of the world back in His glory as His Body is ushered into His presence to be with Him forever.

The Church must not despise prophesies. Instead, they need to be discerned because they might be from God. This might serve as His means to warn and prepare His Body or Church for what is about to come upon it.

Is this one of the predominate gifts you operate in? If so, walk in integrity of heart and in the disposition of humility and sobriety.

---

[5] Matthew 24, Mark 13, Luke 21

If God gives you a prophecy, be faithful to deliver it in meekness according to His perfect timing and trust God to confirm it.

16

TONGUES AND
INTERPRETATION

The next inspirational gift is the gift of tongues. You cannot properly present this gift unless you do so in light of the gift of interpretation.

As previously stated, the gift of tongues is what creates the greatest controversy over the gifts of the Spirit. The reason for this conflict surrounds three issues: 1) control, (2) the Baptism of the Holy Spirit, and (3) the difference between the gift of tongues and the prayer language.

People who encounter the gift of tongues can perceive it as a frightening situation. The strange language initially gives the impression of chaos or insanity to unsuspecting Christians.

I remember taking a friend to an Assembly of God Church. I was aware that the gifts had been in operation in the past, but it seemed minimal. During worship, a person received a message in tongues. As she was speaking forth in this strange language, my concern immediately went out to my friend who never had witnessed the manifestation of the Spirit.

My thought was, "Oh brother, she will probably run out of this church and never look back." Amazingly, she stayed and heard the interpretation of it and remained for the rest of the service. After church, I questioned her. She admitted that her initial response when she heard the strange language was to flee, but the Lord spoke to her and told her that the message was for her.

I can recall that the interpretation of the tongue was that of encouragement, but I had no idea that He was personally reaching out to my friend to minister to her during a difficult and trying time in her life. He not only edified her, but He made me more aware of just how faithful He is to reach out to His people in the most unexpected ways.

My friend actually shared her experience with others and the next Sunday there were more people at church to witness this unusual manifestation. But, true to His sovereign nature, nothing happened. Once again, God confirmed to me that He is not a performer nor does He move just to prove a point to others.

As I have watched people struggle over the gifts of the Holy Spirit, I have wondered why God uses such controversial means to speak forth His truths to His Body, especially the gift of tongues. As I have observed the manifestation of tongues, it struck me that, when this gift manifests, it quickly catches people's attention. When a message comes forth in tongues, it is as if everything stops in great anticipation and everyone's senses are tuned into the very voice of God in readiness to receive from Him.

This is why it is sad that many ignorantly quench this gift because of the need to control even that which is spiritual. Granted, there has been much abuse in the area of the inspirational gifts, but the Church must not do away with a valid work of the Holy Spirit because man has perverted it.

In Christianity, the key to spiritual growth does not lie in personal control, but in personal surrender to the work of the Holy Spirit. The use and reception of gifts is a matter of faith and not a point of personal control or intellectual debate. Instead of believers grieving the Holy Spirit because they limit His work in their midst, they must choose to become discerning and receptive in order to protect His liberty to move as He wills in order to ensure spiritual edification and growth.

The second issue that clouds the gift of tongues is the baptism of the Holy Spirit. Due to the many misconceptions about this subject, it is important to understand this baptism in order to keep it in the proper perspective and avoid unnecessary debates and abuses. For example, there is a debate that the born-again experience is the same as the baptism of the Holy Spirit. If we consider the Scriptures, we will see that there appears to be a distinction between these two experiences.

In John 20:22, we see Jesus giving the Holy Ghost to His disciples before He ascended, "And when he had said this, he breathed on them, and saith unto them, Receive ye the Holy Ghost."

In Luke 24:49, He gave His disciples this promise, "And, behold, I send the promise of my Father upon you: but tarry ye in the city of Jerusalem, until ye be endued with power from on high."

Acts 1:8 states, "But ye shall receive power, after that the Holy Ghost is come upon you: and ye shall be witnesses unto me both in Jerusalem, and in all Judea, and in Samaria, and unto the uttermost part of the earth."

These Scriptures appear to give the impression that the reception of the Holy Ghost upon salvation and the Baptism of the Holy Ghost are two distinct experiences. Keep in mind that the Holy Ghost is referred to as both a gift and promise. He would be given to the believer as a gift upon salvation and a promise upon baptism. The fact that these experiences also end in two different results also implies they are distinct. For example, salvation is the product of the born-again experience where the Spirit of God becomes a resident within the spirit of man. The baptism of the Holy Spirit is an experience that empowers the person to be a bold witness on behalf of Jesus Christ and what He did on the cross for lost man.

As I studied the early Church, I recognized these two experiences were treated as distinct. In fact, the normal practice of the new Church was that, after water baptism (confession of faith), hands were laid upon the individual to receive the Baptism of the Holy Spirit.

According to the information, the laying on of hands for the Baptism of the Holy Ghost was strictly observed for the first 200 years and eventually became a ritual that lost its meaning as it was only allotted to the so-called elite leaders. As a result, it ceased to be a promise to be obtained, but became an unfeeling religious exercise that lost its real purpose or significance.[1] Today, the laying on of hands to receive the Holy Spirit is acknowledged by some in the American Church and is still practiced by those in other countries where adherence to the Word of God is observed in child-like faith and obedience.

I personally believe that, when the power of the Holy Spirit touches His residing presence from within, He becomes the Rivers of Living Water that Jesus made reference to. As the Living Water, He breaks forth from deep within to break down any dams of self, rid of all debris, and bring forth newness of life in power and authority. I believe Scripture confirms this. Jesus said in John 7:37-39, "If any man thirst, let him come unto me, and drink. He that believeth on me, as the scripture hath said, out of his belly shall flow rivers of living water. (But this spake he of the Spirit....)."

John the Baptist made this statement about Jesus in Matthew 3:11, "I indeed baptize you with water unto repentance: but he that cometh after me is mightier than I, whose shoes I am not worthy to bear: he shall baptize you with the Holy Ghost, and with fire."

John the Baptist had been baptizing men in water in light of repentance. In this Scripture verse, he is pointing to a baptism that is solely done by Jesus and is of greater purpose. E. Stanley

---

[1] Deeper Experiences of Famous Christians; by James Gilchrist Lawson; © 2000 by Barbour Publishing, Inc. pg. 47

Jones stated that John's baptism was to get rid of something, while Jesus' baptism is to get possession of the lives of people. He pointed out that water baptism unto repentance died while the baptism of the Holy Spirit lives on. John the Baptist challenged and irritated the religious realm, while Jesus inspired His sheep.[2]

It must be noted that the water baptism that is practiced today is not a sign of repentance, but of identification. The sign of repentance is no longer water baptism, but a changed life.

The controversy over the Baptism of the Holy Spirit escalates when it comes to the evidence of this baptism. Acts 19:6 states, "And when Paul had laid his hands upon them; the Holy Ghost came on them; and they spake with tongues, and prophesied."

It is maintained by a majority of those who believe in the manifestation of the Holy Ghost that the main evidence of this spiritual baptism is speaking in tongues. They back this up with Scriptures such as Acts 2:3-4 and 10:44-48.

This belief often insults those who don't agree with teachings surrounding the Baptism of the Holy Ghost. Obviously, Scripture shows that tongues are evidence of this baptism, but I personally don't believe it is the only evidence. Acts 19:6 also states that the people prophesied as well. We also see that prophecy was the visible evidence manifested after the Spirit of God came upon King Saul in 1 Samuel 10:6 and 19:19-24.

Scripture proves to me that tongues are just one of the signs and not the only sign. Paul reinforced my conclusion by asking the question in 1 Corinthians 12:30, whether all would speak with tongues? I have witnessed in my own life that this baptism brought forth boldness to proclaim my testimony as well as significant change in my life. The Word of God also became more illuminated and personal to me.

---

[2] The Way; Daily devotion, pg. 271

Rayola Kelley

I have also operated in other gifts before I ever spoke in a strange tongue, which brings me to an important question. Can a person display the manifestation of the Spirit without first being baptized with the Holy Ghost?

It is up to each person to explore the Scripture and seek God's perspective on this matter. The truth is that God wants to empower us, not only to victoriously live the Christian life, but to be bold in our witnessing and effective ministers in His kingdom.

As previously stated, the Holy Spirit serves as both a gift and a promise.[3] As a gift, He is given to those upon salvation as a seal to an eternal inheritance and, as a promise, He enables believers to carry out their commission and reach their potential in Christ.

As I have observed the emotional debate over the Baptism of the Holy Ghost and speaking in tongues, I wonder what serves as the greatest point of conflict. It seems both issues are debated with great intensity, but I have to admit it is hard to discern between beliefs driven by pride, ignorance justified by fear, and anger reinforced by the need to control and understand the move and work of God. When you listen to this debate, it becomes obvious that few are seeking for the truth and many are trying to maintain tight reins on their present theology.

No Christian should let the influence of religion and the flesh determine these issues. The responsibility of every Christian is to seek God's perspective through the unbiased study of Scripture and allow Him to establish the proper perception.

The truth about the Holy Spirit is that we need to be constantly filled up with Him.[4] It matters little if we have never experienced His fullness or whether we have; we need to strive to experience the Living Water on a daily basis. My suggestion in this matter is that Christians adhere to Luke 11:13, "If ye then, being evil, know

---

[3] Acts 2:38-39
[4] Ephesians 5:18

137

how to give good gifts unto your children: how much more shall your heavenly Father <u>give the Holy Spirit to them that ask Him</u>?" (Emphasis added.)

The third issue that causes confusion in this area is the difference between the prayer language and the gift of tongues. The Apostle Paul dealt with these two subjects in 1 Corinthians 14:1-6.

Many Christians believe that the gift of tongues and the unknown prayer language are the same. This is a misconception. Just because a person may have a prayer language does not mean they also have the gift of tongues.

I have never operated in the gift of tongues, but I do have a prayer language. Once again, we are reminded by Paul's own words in 1 Corinthians 12:29-30 that not everyone would possess the same gifts, which includes the gift of tongues. Upon questioning those who operate in this gift, they admit that their prayer language is not the same as the tongue they speak with when the gift comes upon them. This would make sense because a person has control over their prayer language, but the gift of tongues would be totally controlled by the Spirit of God. This means the person could utter only that which the Holy Spirit is inspiring.

The gift of tongues and the prayer language also differ according to whom they edify. For example, the gift of tongues must be interpreted which will edify the whole body, while the prayer language mainly edifies the one who prays in it.

There have been situations where people have heard others pray in their native tongue, thereby, being greatly edified. For example, a pastor, through an interpreter, asked a couple of American missionaries who were working in his area to pray for him to be baptized with the Holy Spirit. They laid hands upon him and prayed for him. Within a short time, he began to pray in another tongue. To the missionaries' surprise, his tongue was

English. The Lord used this pastor in his new prayer language to thank the missionaries for their faithful obedience to come to the mission field, and then he began to pray for America.

In another situation, foreign visitors to America were greatly troubled by events surrounding Christians in their native country. When the invitation went out for people to come to the altar to unload their burdens, these Christians went forward to intercede. As they kneeled down by an American, they could hear the person praying in another tongue. To their surprise, the person was praying in their native language. The Lord spoke to them through that person.

Prophetically they were told that He was about to resolve the trouble and for them to take heart. They not only walked away edified, but rejoicing. True to His Word, God took care of this matter in a miraculous way, confirming the message they had heard.

There are many stories about people being ministered to through another person's prayer language. Therefore, this prayer language not only edifies the person who prays in it, but it can touch other people as well.

The prayer language often serves as a shortcut to bring a person past self and personal understanding right into the throne room of God where His will and purpose will be upheld in prayer. Once the person's understanding is out of the way, the Spirit will have the liberty to pray through the person. This is why the prayer language has the ability to offer up unhindered praise, stand in the gap to ensure deliverance, and be used in intercession.

In my own case, I recognize that my personal understanding will often cause repetition of praise, thanksgiving, and requests. By praying in my prayer language all personal boundaries can be quickly brought down as I turn my tongue over to the Spirit. It is from this premise that I can begin to soar in an eternal perspective, bringing edification to my spirit.

The prayer language is great in intercession. I previously mentioned this incident, but it bears mentioning again. The Lord woke a woman up in the middle of the night with a burden for a missionary friend in Africa. She had no idea what was going on, but she sensed the situation was dangerous. The woman began to intercede in her prayer language and continued to do so until the burden lifted. She learned later that the night she was called into intercession for her friend was the night guerrilla fighters took control of the community her friend was ministering in. There were not only bullets flying around, but there was also a possibility of great emotional harm. Throughout the frightening ordeal, God protected the missionary.

Romans 8:26-27 tells us we do not know how to pray, but the Holy Spirit makes intercession for the saints according to the will of God. These intercessions can come out in groanings that cannot be uttered.

This brings us to another aspect of this debate: What does it mean to pray in the Spirit? The Apostle Paul made this statement in Ephesians 6:18, "Praying always with all prayer and supplications in the Spirit, and watching thereunto with all perseverance and supplication for all saints."

I had one individual become furious with me because she had spent hours praying for her family, but it was with her own understanding. She claimed she had been praying in the Spirit. I could not agree with her because of what the Apostle Paul said about this issue in 1 Corinthians 14:14, "For if I pray in an unknown tongue, my spirit prayeth, but my understanding is unfruitful."

As I have studied Scripture, I have not found any other description of praying in the spirit except in this verse, where a person does not understand what is being said. I really do not care if a person agrees or disagrees with my findings, because scriptural understanding should not be a matter of who is right or wrong, but rather the willingness to line up with God's Word about a subject.

The Apostle Paul went on to say, "I will pray with the spirit, and I will pray with the understanding also" (1 Corinthians 14:15). Again, Paul made a distinction between praying with the Spirit and praying with understanding in his own tongue.

However, the Holy Spirit can impact prayers in three ways: 1) He can *inspire* a person to pray for something specific; 2) He can *lead* an individual to pray because of a burden; or 3) He can *anoint* a person in their prayers to bring about a desired result. If the Holy Spirit is involved in our prayers in any way, we can be assured that they will have power before the throne and will hit the mark.

Now that the distinction between the prayer language and the gift of tongues has been discussed, it is time to consider how the gift of tongues operates. According to the Apostle Paul in 1 Corinthians 14:22, the gift of tongues initially serves as a sign to them who do not believe. The fact that tongues serve as a sign to unbelievers is confirmed by what Mark 16:17 stated, "And these signs shall follow them that believe: In my name shall they cast out devils; they shall speak with new tongues."

This confirmation was evident on the day of Pentecost. Those in the upper room were given many different tongues, and, as a result, the Gospel touched many people of different languages.[5]

When the gift of tongues is in proper operation within the Body, it can have words of knowledge, wisdom (revelation), or prophecy that will reveal the mysteries of God.[6]

This means God may be instructing, warning, encouraging, or giving direction to a person or the body through this gift. This is why this gift must not be forbidden as long as it is inspired by the right spirit and within scriptural boundaries.

---

[5] Acts 2
[6] 1 Corinthians 14:1, 6

1 Corinthians 14:27-28 clearly states that there must not be more than three messages in tongues in a meeting, and each message must be interpreted. In fact, the person who speaks in tongues is instructed to pray for the interpretation of it.[7]

This brings us to another point of conflict. There is so much suspicion in regards to this gift. Skeptics have a tendency to question the validity of a tongue that is interpreted by the same person. On the other hand, I have sensed in a couple of incidents where both tongues and interpretation were staged between two different people. This proves that everything must be discerned on the basis of spirit, and not according to one's feelings or beliefs.

Are you personally open to this gift? Does God want to use you in this area or are you unwilling to even go there because of concrete doctrine, fear, or ignorance?

Gift of Interpretation

The gift of interpretation is the gift that verifies the gift of tongues and ensures that the whole body will be edified. The gift of tongues may get our attention, but interpretation is like turning on the light to bring understanding and enlightenment to people.

The gift of interpretation is not a true form of translation that is word for word of a message, but the means of conveying the spirit, intent, and meaning behind the message. For instance, there was a message in tongues and interpretation in a church I was attending. The actual message of tongues was short, but the interpretation was lengthy. The pastor who interpreted the message reminded the congregation that interpretation was not a word for word translation.

This is the one inspirational gift I operate in the most. I can tell you from experience that to operate in one of the inspirational gifts

---

[7] 1 Corinthians 14:13

is like stepping off of a cliff and hoping God will be there to meet you.

In my first experience of interpretation of tongues, I missed the opportunity because of fear and inexperience. There was a message in tongues and I felt heat rushing up my body. Four words ran across my mind like a ticker tape. I asked God for more words to ensure I was receiving the interpretation, but the four same words kept running across my mind.

I struggled in the silence as I wrestled with this new experience. I did not want to open my mouth and speak only four words and then be left up in the air, looking like an immature fool. After much silence, a prophecy came forth, allowing me to justify my silence and fear as well as let off a sigh of relief that I had remained quiet. Just as I was about to pat myself on the back for restraint, another person opened her mouth and the same four words that had run across my mind came out in boldness and authority.

The woman who was overseeing the meeting took time out to instruct us about gifts. To this day, I appreciate her sensitivity to the struggle and her willingness to share her experiences in the area of gifts to bring proper instruction.

In my years of being a Christian, I have only met two other individuals besides the instructor who took time out of the meeting to properly instruct the saints about this subject. Today I still consider these people gems.

There are so many people who secretly struggle with the gifts, especially the inspirational gifts. These gifts require a measure of faith to step out in obedience to participate in something strange and uncomfortable. The possibilities of looking foolish in the process can be overwhelming to the inexperienced and uncertain vessel. But, as I am often reminded, faith begins where understanding ceases.

I don't know how many times I have wrestled over the gift of interpretation. I have wondered if it is my imagination, yet I never know what I am going to say past the four words that I am initially given. Out of faith, I open my mouth and speak what I see until the words cease.

I remember when, in one interpretation, I was clipping along as I was speaking forth the combination of words and pictures. All of a sudden, the words came to an abrupt end as if I stopped in the middle of a sentence. Of course, it was not the middle of the sentence, but my momentum was still at high speed. I realize God used that situation to show me that it was not my imagination, but a true manifestation of His Spirit.

I have even argued with God about the gift of interpretation. In a firm voice, He put me in my place when He said, "I can take it away from you." I realize that not only would I be burying a gift, but I also was failing God and His Body. I quickly repented.

Over the years, I have learned to wait for a few seconds before giving the interpretation as a means to confirm to me whether or not I have the interpretation. Even after years of experience, I still have some anxiety when God gives me the interpretation of a tongue. However, as I talk to others who operate in these different gifts, I have discovered this anxiety is not unusual when it comes to the function of these gifts.

I have also found the gift of interpretation can be used in interpreting visions or dreams and explaining mysteries or hidden treasure that can be found in parables or proverbs. We see this ability to interpret visions and dreams in the lives of Joseph and Daniel.[7] In my own situation, I have been used in the interpretation of visions and dreams and, always in a state of awe, I have watched some come true.

---

[7] Genesis 40:5; Daniel 2:4; Proverbs 1:6

Do you have the gift of interpretation or are you closing it down because of fear and the lack of instruction? Be willing to open yourself up and take the step of faith and allow the Holy Spirit the freedom to minister to the Body through you.

17

THE CHALLENGE

As I struggle with my conclusion to this book, I have to recognize that God did establish an incredible pattern to bring about edification in the Body. This pattern has been carefully laid out and recorded, yet His Body debates and quibbles over how to interpret it. As a result, much of the Body picks and chooses according to indoctrination and not scriptural instruction.

2 Timothy 3:16 tells us **all** Scripture is inspired and given to establish doctrine, and it is to be used for personal reproof, correction, and instruction in righteousness. Yet, how many Christians consider all Scriptures as being from God and the only means of substantiating righteous attitudes, pure doctrine, and godly lifestyles? Sadly, the percentage of Christians that approach the Bible with the correct perspective is dangerously low.

Much of the scriptural debate that is going on is not a matter of standing for truth, but a platform on which religious pride is exalted, ignorance is covered by a cloak of religious zeal, and fear is hidden behind skepticism and theological discussion. I do not have a problem when people admit they do not understand certain aspects of the Bible. My main complaint rests with people who change, ignore, or do away with Bible truths because of pride, fear, or ignorance.

It is up to each person to make a choice. Either the entire Bible is true or none of it is true. It is not up to mere man to determine what is acceptable in it or try to justify it by influencing others to follow in his spiritual causes. It is one thing to admit personal challenges over a scriptural teaching, but it is another matter to stand in the way of other people seeking out God's perspective.

When will the Body of Christ learn that God's truths do not come down to what is considered popular or accepted theology of man any more than God's works must be considered in light of what is comfortable? God's truths and works never will come down to man's fleshly or religious perspective, but to what God wants to accomplish in and through His people. This work has an eternal purpose that mere man is unable to grasp except by faith.

Subsequently, the debate in the Church does not find its origins in doctrine, but in unbelief. Many Christians have allowed others to define their beliefs. These assumed beliefs are nothing more than idolatrous in nature and, wherever idolatry exists, there is unbelief towards the real truths of God.

God has clearly established a pattern and avenues by which the Body is to be edified. The first pattern is found in the leadership in Ephesians 4:11. This leadership is to serve as a visible expression of Jesus' disposition—servitude and total commitment to the building of His Church and kingdom for the glory of God.

In Romans 12:5-8, we see a diverse Body that is to be a physical extension of Christ as it serves in humility and reaches out in benevolence. This extension of Jesus is not only for the edification of the Body to bring it to maturity, but it is also to reach out to the lost in example, sensitivity, and sacrificial ways.

This brings us to the gifts of the Spirit found in 1 Corinthians 12 and 14. These are the gifts that have been done away with in so many different denominations. They are treated as if they hinge or depend on man when the Scripture states that these gifts are a manifestation of the Holy Spirit.

The Holy Spirit's main responsibility is to lift Jesus up, but He does have one area in which He manifests His sovereignty and

147

supernatural works—the supernatural gifts. These gifts are either being denounced, accredited to Satan, or they are being abused in such a way that they give the Holy Spirit a spiritual black eye.

My scriptural understanding is that the Church needs the intervention and work of all three Persons of the Godhead. Each person of the Godhead is necessary, and to do away with any work or manifestation of them is to do away with the complete work of salvation and edification.

2 Corinthians 13:14 states, "The grace of the Lord Jesus Christ, and the love of God, and the communion of the Holy Ghost, be with you all. Amen." In this verse, we are reminded that Christ's death on the cross was an act of grace that secures our salvation.

As we consider the love of God, we know this is in reference to the love of the Father, "Behold, what manner of love the Father hath bestowed upon us, that we should be called the sons of God: therefore the world knoweth us not, because it knew him not" (1 John 3:1).

Jesus' death on the cross established a new covenant wherein God's people would be known as children of God. This would point to an intimate relationship with God, but this relationship is only made possible by the communion of the Holy Ghost.

The Holy Spirit reproves, seals, guides, and sanctifies. He is the One who moves upon, in, and through God's people. He is the one who unites and edifies the Body of Christ. He is the one who ensures the sacrifice of praise and opens the door of worship for sweet communion. Yet, few know the third Person of the Godhead enough to be able to discern His presence, work, and manifestation.

As a result of this lack of intimacy with the Holy Spirit, there are two extremes: 1) Those who do away with His work; therefore, keeping Him abstract instead of personal and, 2) those who accredit everything supernatural and spiritual to Him, making Him appear foolish and ridiculous.

There is a proper presentation and balance when it comes to the Person of the Holy Spirit and His work, but that balance can only be found in the Word of God. Sadly, it is often explained away. People, who cling to doctrines will close down, ignore, or abuse those areas of the Bible instead of seeking to know God's perspective about His Spirit and the work He does.

Each individual will be responsible for how they handle the third person of the Godhead. Each will be held accountable if they bury any of His gifts or grieve, quench, resist or reject Him.

This brings us back to the gifts of the Spirit. As you study these gifts, you cannot help but notice that the Holy Spirit remains true to form in them. We see through these gifts that the Holy Spirit is powerful, but remains a quiet servant as God's plans, heart, and intent are revealed to the Body. He remains gentle as faith is given, discernment is added, and wisdom is unveiled. He gives way as Christ is exalted in worship and moves in the body as its members are warned, encouraged, instructed, and ministered to.

It is easy to declare that these gifts have ceased until a person encounters their operation. It is convenient to ignore them until there is a testimony of their importance. It is justifiable to accredit them to other sources besides the third Person of the Godhead until one comes face to face with their supernatural ability to change lives.

To close down this avenue of edification is a great loss for the Church. In spite of the abuses, I have seen the Holy Ghost manifest Himself, and, in doing so, I have witnessed obstacles fleeing, hearts changed, and heaven revealed.

As I weigh the pros and cons of these different means of edification, I have concluded that I would rather risk and confront the improper use of them than close down the means by which God's Spirit can move.

I want to encourage believers to put aside pet theologies and seek God's face about this matter. My desire for this search is not to prove a point, but my desire is that Christians will find their proper place in the Body of Christ and be used effectively in the work of edification.

I believe that it is vital for the days we live in that every blood-bought saint is in their proper position in the Body and operating with the gift or gifts the Holy Spirit wants to allocate to them. It is of little concern to me what position or gift a believer has, but what does matter to me is that the Church will properly function in a powerful way for the glory of God.

The question is how does one find their place in the Body of Christ? It is simple. Go to the Father and ask Him to give you the life He has for you. This means asking for more of His life, which means you will be asking Him for more of His Spirit. Ask Him to also equip you to be effective in the Church and to give you boldness to work in the harvest field. Once the Father gives you more of His life, make sure you go to Jesus daily to ask to be filled up with His Living Water.

The power and anointing of the Holy Spirit are vital, especially as darkness is about to engulf this world. The Church needs to be healthy so that it can serve as the salt of the earth and the light of the world in order to penetrate the darkness for the sake of searching souls.

The question is will you seek the reality of this powerful life? Will you accept the challenge to put aside religious boundaries and seek the life and perspective of God about all matters? After all, how you handle God's truths comes down to whether or not you want to possess everything He has for you in spite of what you personally believe or perceive.

BIBLIOGRAPHY

Strong's Exhaustive Concordance of the Bible; James Strong, ©
    1986 assigned to World Bible Publishers, Inc
Webster's New Collegiate Dictionary; © 1976 by G. & C.
    Merriam Co.
Encyclopedia of Sermon Illustrations; ©1988 Concordia
    Publishing House
Deeper Experience Of Famous Christians; by James Gilchrist
    Lawson; © 2000 by Barbour Publishing Inc.
The Way; (Devotional) by Stanley Jones © 1946 by Stone &
    Pierce
A Dwelling Place For God; by Ruth Specter Lascelle; © 1990 by
    Hyman Israel Specter, Van Nuys CA.
Will the Real Heretics Please Stand Up; © 1989, 3RD edition, ©
    1999 by David W. Bercot
The Gifts of the Spirit; by Harold Horton, © 1934

Volume Six: Developing Our Christian Life
The Many Faces of Christianity
*Possessing Our Souls
Experiencing the Christian Life
The Power of Our Testimonies
*The Victorious Journey

Devotions
Devotions of the Heart: Books One and Two
Daily Food for the Soul: Books One and Two

Gentle Shepherd Ministries Devotion Series:
Being a Child of God
Disciplining the Strength of our Youth
Coming to Full Age

Nugget Books:
Nuggets From Heaven
More Nuggets From Heaven
Heavenly Gems
More Heavenly Gems
Heavenly Treasures
More Heavenly Treasures

Gentle Shepherd Ministries Series:

The Christian Life Series
What Matter Is This?
The Challenge of It
The Reality of It

The Leadership Series
Overcoming
A Matter of Authority and Power
The Dynamics of True Leadership

Books By:
Jeannette Haley
Books co-authored with Rayola Kelley:
Hidden Manna (original)
The Many Faces of Christianity (Volume 6)
Post to Post 3: Meditations Along the Way
Post to Post 4: Inspirations Along the Way
Post to Post 5: Collecting Gems Along the Way

Other Books:
Rose of Light, Thorn of Darkness
Interview In Hell}
Interview On Earth}
(Both Interview Books are now in one book
Angelus Assignments)
The Pig and I
Reflections of Wonder (Devotional)

Children's Books:
Little Stories for Little People
Traveler's Tales
The Adventures of Zack and Mira
The Adventures of Paul and Dana
(A House on the Beach)
The Monster of Mystery Valley

*Books that have been separated from the volumes and are now available under their own titles.

www.ingramcontent.com/pod-product-compliance
Lightning Source LLC
Chambersburg PA
CBHW072150090426
42740CB00012B/2212